Abuse of rank is epidemic.

- In their careers, 37% of workers are bullied by colleagues and superiors.
- Each year, parents and guardians mistreat and neglect nearly a million children.
- Of over a half million abused elderly, 85% of the abuse occurs at the hands of family members.
- As many as 12% of girls are sexually abused.
- One in four children admit to being school bullies, and one in five say they both bully and have been bullied. (See Preface for Sources)

*"A practical guide to successfully defending oneself against the abuses of rank that crop up in most everyone's personal relationships and public lives, Dr. Wambach's book is user-friendly, handy, and full of common sense. It is illustrated with rich, concrete examples that readers will be able to apply to their own situations and so better protect themselves from the indignities of rankism."*

— ROBERT W. FULLER, AUTHOR OF *SOMEBODIES AND NOBODIES: OVERCOMING THE ABUSE OF RANK AND ALL RISE: SOMEBODIES, NOBODIES AND THE POLITICS OF DIGNITY*

*"Julie Wambach has compiled an impressive typology of rankism. If you want to understand what rankism means, what devastating effects it can have, and how to fight it-this is the book you want to read!"*

— NOA ZANOLLI DAVENPORT, CO-AUTHOR OF *MOBBING: EMOTIONAL ABUSE IN THE AMERICAN WORKPLACE*

OCT 2008

# Battles between Somebodies and Nobodies

# Battles between Somebodies and Nobodies:

## Stop Abuse of Rank at Work and at Home

### Julie Ann Wambach, Ph.D.

*Foreword by Robert W. Fuller*
*Illustrations by Rita van Alkemade*

**Brookside Press**
**Scottsdale, Arizona**

Published by
Brookside Press
P.O. Box 12244, Scottsdale, AZ 85267
*right-rank.com*

For book orders:
BookMasters, Inc.
P.O. Box 388
Ashland OH 44805
800-247-6553
*order@BookMasters.com*

Illustrations by Rita van Alkemade

Author photograph by Morton Rosenberg

Library of Congress Control Number: 2008900556

ISBN: 978-0-9814818-0-7

The author wishes readers to use and benefit from the information
included herein, but to know that this book is no substitute for the
services of a professional. The author and publishers assume no liability
or responsibility to anyone or any entity for alleged damages caused
directly or indirectly from information included in this book.

*For*

*Rick,*

*my toughest critic, who for forty-some years has
been my best friend and champion of my work,*

*and*

*Terri and Bobbi,*

*our daughters, who fill us with endless pride.*

*"I would hope that the world would realize that there is no situation that is not transfigurable, that there is no situation of which we can say, 'This is absolutely, totally devoid of hope.'"*

—Desmond Tutu, on *The Bill Moyers Show,* about South Africa's Truth and Reconciliation Commission Report

# CONTENTS

# FOREWORD

In *Battles between Somebodies and Nobodies*, Dr. Julie Wambach has advanced the analysis of rankism and dignity in two important ways. First, she has amplified the notion of rankism—abuse of the power that attaches to rank—by providing numerous down-to-earth examples drawn from all walks of life; and second, she gives many practical, often brilliant, suggestions as to how to overcome rankism-in our own personal lives, at work, and in the world.

By introducing the notion of "right-rank," Dr. Wambach has clarified the crucial distinction between rank and rankism: namely the difference between legitimate rank—that is rank rightly used—and the illegitimate use of rank, to diminish or exploit others. Throughout this insightful and timely book, she never loses sight of the fact that good leadership is inseparable from treating everyone, regardless of their place in the hierarchy, with dignity. Paradoxically, *Battles between Somebodies and Nobodies* is a book about how to avoid doing battle: Instead of aiming to return an indignity that someone may have inflicted on you, it is about standing up for yourself without harming others, even and especially if they have harmed you. Only in this way, is the cycle of vengeance broken. Only as we learn to protect the dignity of others, do we create the dignitarian world that is humankind's common destiny.

In sum, *Battles between Somebodies and Nobodies* goes a long way to replacing the battles we have all participated in with the peaceful resolutions we require to build a world of equal dignity for all in the 21st century. Dignity is an idea whose time is near, and Dr. Wambach has brought that day closer.

—Robert W. Fuller, former president of Oberlin College, and author of *Somebodies and Nobodies: Overcoming the Abuse of Rank* and *All Rise: Somebodies, Nobodies, and the Politics of Dignity*

# PREFACE

A television network news program recounted an experiment its staff had conducted with hidden cameras.[1] Reporters wanted to see how people respond to a live incident of verbal abuse against a child. Two actors, a twenty-something woman and an eight-year-old boy, enacted a drama between a youngster and his caretaker. As the boy sat with head lowered and shoulders slumped, the woman shouted a litany of reasons that he was awful—such as he was stupid, he was terrible to be with, he was a burden to his mother, and he would never amount to anything. The baby-sitter often went on for twenty or thirty minutes in a variety of settings—golf course, city park, playground—most likely to attract bystanders.

While several adults did stop to watch, almost no one interceded. Not one man stopped. When asked why, the men gave the same reasons as most women who did not stop. They thought someone else would do it. Besides, they were not sure if it was their place to butt in.

Of those few women who did come forward, all had small children and said they felt compelled to help the child. Only one woman made a broader connection. She was a mother who once saw a man beat a woman and did nothing to help. She often wondered what had happened to the beaten woman.

The mother admitted she was shaking when she approached the baby-sitter but resolved to do the right thing this time.

That mother had more than courage. She had the realization that physical abuse of a spouse or partner is equivalent to verbal abuse of a child. She likely did not know the word "rankism," but she made the association this book advocates.

Rankism, the abuse of position within a hierarchy, is the core of all mistreatment, regardless of context. Rankism is an umbrella for every sort of abuse you can think of. Huddled under the rankism umbrella are reasons one set of people discriminates against another group. While some details of a specific abuse situation can be unique, the dynamics of all mistreatment, all discrimination, are remarkably similar.

I remember the day I heard Robert W. Fuller on *The Diane Rhem Show* talking about his book on rankism. As soon as the interview finished, I headed for the closest bookstore and purchased Fuller's book. Returning to the parking lot, I rolled down my car windows and read the book straight through. I knew immediately that he had unearthed a basic truth about our injury of one another: all abuse is based on misuse of position. I knew that Fuller's book, *Somebodies and Nobodies: Overcoming the Abuse of Rank,* was the seminal book on rankism. It was in the tradition of Rachel Carson's *Silent Spring,* which foreshadowed the ecology movement, and Betty Friedan's *Feminine Mystique,* which set the stage for the feminist movement.

Within the month, I began writing this book. Early on, I was intrigued that a rankism perspective toward communication interplay offered me such a wealth of understanding. Perhaps, because I grew up in a German-American family with a strong hierarchical structure. Perhaps, because I taught human interaction dynamics for over thirty years. Perhaps, because I always had trouble taking orders—especially from those who barked at me. For some reason, I have always been aware of who had what type of power within each communication event. With a new rankism lens, I could better see what might go wrong among people.

As I continued to study and write, I realized how my book, *Battles between Somebodies and Nobodies: Stop Abuse of Rank at Work and at Home* built on Fuller's work. I noticed that among those atop hierarchies as well as those further down, there was always someone who managed to misuse his or her position. I wanted us all to recognize rankism, refuse to accept rankism, and to hold ourselves and others accountable for the way we treat one another. Most of all, I wanted to provide specific ways for us to stop rankism.

For, rankism is epidemic. The U.S. Department of Health and Human Services estimated that each year nearly a million children are mistreated or neglected and over half a million elderly abused—85% of them by family members. According to the National Coalition for Child Protection and Reform, as many as 12% of girls are sexually abused. The U.S. Department of Education reported that one in four children admitted to being a school bully and one in five said they both bullied and had been bullied. According to a Zogby International survey 37% of American workers have been bullied.[2]

These numbers, staggering as they are, are brought home by accounts from individual targets of rankism. Some stories included in this book were published elsewhere and I tell you how to find the originals. Others were either observed by me or related to me by those involved. If an anecdote clarifies a point, I consider it worth sharing. Some stories are compilations in which I carefully changed all names and identifying information except for my own. If I expect others to face their own rankism, I need to share mine. So, you will be reading about times when I, too, was a rankist.

There are examples here of political figures who have grossly misused their positions, as well as regular folks like you and me. I use public examples because they make my point. This is not a book, however, about the political ramifications of rankism; in his own books, Bob Fuller presents those very well. I concentrate on the interpersonal aspects of rankism. My goal is to usher you along a path toward right-rank, a stance where you treat others with dignity—regardless of their rank—and demand the same of everyone in your world.

The book chapters provide all the signposts you will need to follow along the road to right-rank. Each chapter ends with exercises you can do to help you reach right-rank and stop rankism in your life. Part I introduces you to rankism and what does and does not make hierarchies work well. Part II looks at why we humans strike at those of different rank. Part III introduces you to a number of Somebody Rankists, and Nobody Rankists, as well as a couple Nobodies of right-rank. Part IV shows how you can put all this information together to stop rankism in any part of your life.

So, let us begin our journey to right-rank. If you find anything here that raises questions or that you would like to comment on, go to my website *www.right-rank.com*. I would love to hear from you.

# Battles between Somebodies and Nobodies

## Part One

# Rankism Happens

Chapters One and Two introduce you to the basics of rankism so you can begin on your path to right-rank. Hierarchies are the context within which rankism occurs. Within these assemblies of unequals, we all bear the potential for misusing our positions. If you have not been aware of all the hierarchies of which you are a part, this discussion should peak your curiosity. Hierarchies are the framework within which rankism abides, but they are not the problem. The problem is that we *create* Somebodies and Nobodies, and that leads to cycles of rankism.

*Rankism.* Robert W. Fuller coined the word "rankism" to describe the misuse of position by those in power when they mistreat individuals who are less forceful. Fuller described how we all have felt the sting of abuse by those higher up the status ladder and how this abuse by Somebodies negatively affects our lives and society. Fuller also proposed that Nobodies assemble to overcome rankism. I go further in saying that higher-ups and those down the ladder can misuse their positions and hurt others.

*Hierarchies.* We arrange ourselves into social hierarchies with individuals of higher and lower ranks. Like other species, we have some good reasons for creating systems with various ranks. All of this works pretty well so long as people use their rank to better all those concerned. Those who misuse their rank position harm individuals and the work of groups.

*Somebodies and Nobodies.* While all social animals organize into hierarchies, only humans go so far as to create Somebodies and Nobodies. Somebodies know they are important because those around them treat them with respect and dignity. Human beings become Nobodies when they are belittled, put down, ignored, or otherwise abused. That abuse comes from a rankist, a person misusing a position.

Everyone encounters rankism. Both Somebodies and Nobodies have the power to make ranking systems work well if they treat one another decently.

*Cycles of rankism.* At some time or another, we have all been mistreated by a rankist. That is why we all know so much about rank. We are all guilty of misusing both lead positions and follower positions because the dynamics within a particular system caused us hurt. Somebodies may abuse Nobodies who, in turn, strike back. This conflict between Somebodies and Nobodies occurs in families, businesses, churches/synagogues/mosques, schools, political parties, service organizations, friendship groups—anywhere that people organize themselves.

## CHAPTER ONE

# *We Reside in Hierarchies*

You are about to start a journey toward a better world for yourself and everyone else. We will be heading toward a place where you insist that others treat you and everyone else with respect. This is not a pie-in-the-sky dream I am proposing. Your life can be free of bullies, verbal and physical abusers, and anyone who puts you down. Your life without rankism—the abuse of position within a hierarchy—can happen.

We begin with hierarchies, the way we arrange ourselves so everyone is on different levels. Some are above us and some are below. These hierarchies have a profound effect on how we deal with others. As is often the case, we can each learn more about ourselves by looking at others. Let us begin with other social beings, those of the nonhuman, animal world. They have much to teach us.

## Hierarchies in Animal Societies

The creatures with which we share this planet organize themselves into hierarchies or orders of rank. We refer to top dogs and underdogs, or Alphas and Omegas. Alpha means top because it is the first letter of the Greek alphabet. Within hierarchies, any creature might be Alpha or Beta or Delta or somewhere down the line, a Sigma or Tau—all Greek letters. Omega animals (or humans) are those with the least power because Omega is the last letter of the Greek alphabet.

*Birds do it.* Endangered whooping cranes, raised in captivity so they can be reintroduced to the wild, must learn to get along with their kind. Upon leaving their birthing cages, the young whooping cranes settle one another into lines that become their flying order when they follow a human-piloted ultralight on their first migration from Canada to Texas. Hummingbirds at a feeder where several hummers gather often have one Alpha hummer who controls traffic and decides who can drink and when. Chickens create pecking orders in the farmyard. Cocks even fight one another to a bloody death in order to establish dominance.

*Bees do it.* In a beehive, each insect knows its place. The drones fuss over the queen bee and the worker bees collect the pollen and make honey. In an ant colony, there is one queen and many workers who have a single task—tend the young, secure food, take out the trash, or protect the colony. Some ants even steal pupae—ant children—from other nests and turn them into slaves.

*Wild things do it.* Wolf packs and lion prides have a leader who determines who can mate, who cares for the young, who hunts, and who eats first. Baboon Alphas ruthlessly enforce their place at the top of the group.

*Domestic animals do it.* Cats. Yes, cats. Ask humans who share their homes with more than one cat and they will tell you which of the cats is Alpha and how he or she rules the other cats. Hierarchies are the basis for training domestic animals. The animal trainer becomes the top dog, top cat, top horse, top bird, top lion. How? The trainer's personal demeanor and control of food ensures who will be Alpha.

## Hierarchies among Humans

As with other species, we have good reasons for creating rank-based systems. Much of our world is arranged in hierarchies.[1] Even among countries, there are different hierarchies. The military strength of a superpower like the United States is far stronger than that of France. French culinary arts exceed those of England. English pageantry surpasses anything in the United States. We could select numerous types of hierarchy to study, but in this book we will concentrate on social ranks: how individuals within groups organize themselves above and below one another.

Employing hierarchies in our treatment of one another starts early. Children play "Follow the Leader," where one youngster leads others through a series of actions and the rest of us must follow suit. Wave arms or dance in circles. Pull your lips across a protruded tongue and cross your eyes. Tiptoe across the grass then fall limp into the fragrant green coverage. If Jimmy does his stupid yodeling thing, we will all have to try that weird noise. If Melanie shows off her athleticism by walking on the wall, we will give it a go. As they get older, kids find that "King of the Mountain" whets their appetite to be in charge. The King (and sometimes Queen) defends the mountain and, one by one, we try to remove him from his place of prominence.

These games teach us that we must find our place as leaders and followers. Sometimes we are at the top and sometimes we challenge those above us.

When people use rank for the betterment of all concerned, our relationships, families, workplaces, and the world are better for it. However, when rank is misused, it harms individuals and the goals of groups.

*Explicit and ambiguous hierarchies.* Some hierarchies are open and explicit. Government bureaucracies divide into formal departments with heads who give orders to middle managers who oversee their workers. In an elementary school, eighth graders have more prestige than do fifth graders who boss second graders.

An organizational chart shows clearly how a business depicts itself. The president and board are the Alphas. The managers below them, down to the rank and file at the bottom, are the Omegas. Organizational charts are usually very open. Everyone who joins the business quickly becomes aware of who is accountable to whom by way of an organizational chart. Those who do business with the company also receive organizational charts.

Consider the following example. The chart at right shows only a portion of a complex organization's hierarchy. Within each department (for example, Mgr. TV Adv.) there would be a further breakdown.

While some more formal hierarchies are explicit, other hierarchies are ambiguous. These hierarchies are less obvious, somewhat fuzzy, and more difficult to figure out. Hierarchies can defy our expectations. For example, it would seem natural for us to predict that the bigger and more outgoing youngster will become the Alpha. Yet, the Alphas in a group may also turn out to be small, introverted kids with musical or computer skills. We expect parents to be the Alphas. What happens when a pampered princess, whose parents throw parties and shower

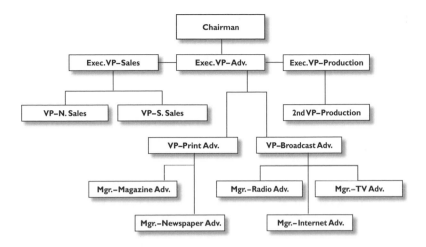

gifts and attention upon her peers, becomes the Alpha? Her parents could find themselves in the position of becoming the daughter's Omega servants. Ambiguous hierarchies can defy our first impressions. We may know the boss is Alpha, always in charge when in the room. What we notice later is that when the boss is away, it is the administrative assistant who decides who in the organization receives consideration and even funding for projects. Ambiguous hierarchies can be very subtle. While there may be no designated leader within a friendship group, there are always Alphas and Omegas. To determine which is which, you may have to watch closely to see who speaks first, who has everyone's attention when making a suggestion. Ambiguous hierarchies are much more complicated because the people involved can move around depending on the situation or topic. In traditional marriages, the husband controlled the money issues and the wife controlled the household issues. Today, we cannot predict which partner will watch the money or if each will handle their own.

*Assorted daily hierarchies.* Janelle is a nineteen-year-old who knows her dentist, Peter, is Alpha while she sits in the dental chair at his office. Yet after work, when Peter heads for the gym where Janelle is a trainer (the Alpha) and he is somewhere down the line of athletic prowess, their roles are reversed.

While animal and human hierarchies share some similarities, we humans are a particularly complex social species. Cranes, hummingbirds, wolves, and horses tend to stay within one or a few groups. We move from one life scene to another throughout most days. In each of those scenes, we reside in a different hierarchy. At home, we may be the Alpha parent or caretaker. At work, instead of being the leader, we may be located further down the hill in a Beta or Lambda position. As a longtime volunteer, you may be the Alpha who knows where everything is stored, the person everyone comes to when they need answers. When we enter a new social situation, one of our first tasks is to determine who the Alphas are and where we and everyone else fits in. That includes those in the middle and bottom of the hierarchy.

*Choice of hierarchies.* As you take the journey toward right-rank—where everyone treats others with respect—remember that you have more choices than you may have first considered.

In the United States, we have sufficient control of our lives to sometimes take the Alpha rank. Sometimes we elect to be further down the line. Unlike some parts of our world where there are those who are always at the bottom of the social and economic heap, in America it is commonplace for people to proceed from one hierarchy to another into various positions that can function smoothly for themselves and for the respective groups.

**Stay and revise, or move on.** Clint worked as an insurance agent for nearly forty years. He often talked about a time when he was going to change professions. Clint believed that if customers faithfully paid their premiums, the company was responsible to be there for those customers when they had a claim. The national company for which he worked had created a complicated system for preventing payment. If Clint acted on his conscience, the national vice president berated him for not following procedures that would evade fair settlement.

So Clint joined a new company, one with a very different policy. Heads of this insurance company assumed their obligations to honor customer contracts. Clint could now carefully explain each plan and what the customer should expect.

Clint had decided that he did not want to bother trying to change the first company he worked for, so he chose to move.

There may be times when the best you can do is move on to a different hierarchy. There are places where maybe the climate is against us. If you are a woman and the hierarchy insists that only men can hold positions of influence, you may want to move. If your religious beliefs put you at variance with those who determine dogma, you may want to leave. If your sexual preference is held against you in any hierarchy, you may want to find a more compatible environment. If your family dynamics are worse than you can endure, you may want to leave. Our time on earth is short and you may decide to get on with your life.

Maxine moved away from her town and later returned. She told me the trouble with moving away was that she could not find a better place. You may decide you are where you want to be. This is your relationship, your family, your workplace, and your community. If you decide you care enough about making revisions, this book can offer you ways to do that. If you decide you have no other place to go, this book will help you create a plan for revisions. Whether to stay and revise the way others use a hierarchy is a choice only you can make.

*Unplanned rank changes.* When you stay within a hierarchy, you have the option to change your rank. George, who worked with others to set up a baseball team, was surprised when his new teammates kept looking to him for direction. Where do we practice? When? Who plays which position? What is our batting order? Without expecting it, George found himself being treated as team manager. He liked to play ball, but had never meant to be team leader. He admitted his change in rank kind of delighted him, and made him nervous.

*Planned rank changes.* More often, we do our best and decide when we want to change—either up or down—within a hierarchy. When her first child was born, Nina decided to take a different job within her company. She wanted to stay home with the baby and work part time. To make this change, Nina knew she would have to turn over most of her accounts to a colleague. It was not until she set up her home office and worked away from her former colleagues that Nina realized how much her position had been diminished. In a short time, she decided that the change was fine, and she had made the right decision.

We understand that we cannot move into a new arena and immediately take charge. We pay our dues before we move up. The problems of rankism come when Alphas are Somebodies, and when the Omegas or Gammas or Deltas are treated as Nobodies.

## Somebodies and Nobodies

While it is usual for us to refer to ranks within animal and human groups as Alpha and Omega, humans residing in hierarchies are more than Greek letters. Some in each hierarchy become Somebodies, and some can become Nobodies.

*More and less than Alphas and Omegas.* Webmasters have offered sites where teens can rate their teachers and comment on other students. Words such as "snot," "ugly," and "worst ever" have been affixed to names of actual students and teachers. One board received four hundred postings a day from anonymous contributors. Parents were concerned about the effect these negative postings would have on youngsters who were so belittled. Some worried that one of the targeted teens might retaliate with physical violence. Those opposed to the site had trouble finding a way to stop the sites.[2] We sometimes treat one another in ways that diminish a person's human worth. Just as Alphas become the powerful members in animal groups, so the Omegas may become the downtrodden and oppressed. This mistreatment of others is for no reason other than that they are considered to be of a higher or lower rank. By the time they are teens, adolescents know a lot about rankism.

*Who are Somebodies and Nobodies?* Somebodies and Nobodies are defined by feelings. When someone up the line treats us badly, we feel as though our personal worth is assaulted. When someone treats us with respect, we become a Somebody. Stephanie Heuer wrote a children's book entitled *I Feel Like a Nobody When… I Feel Like a Somebody When….*[3] She used children's phrases as they completed those two sentences. The young people recalled that they felt like Somebodies when they felt appreciated, recognized, and responsible within their families and school classes. They wanted the same treatment adults want. Stephanie's students were also able to offer immediate instances when they felt hurt, humiliated, or harassed—in other words, like Nobodies.

Compare the feelings we can attach to those who feel like Somebodies and those who feel like Nobodies.

| Somebodies feel | Nobodies feel |
|-----------------|----------------|
| Noticed | Overlooked |
| Encouraged | Discouraged |
| Welcomed | Spurned |
| Appreciated | Depreciated |
| Respected | Disrespected |
| Included | Excluded |
| Esteemed | Shamed |
| Acclaimed | Disdained |
| Elevated | Demeaned |
| Loved | Despised |

Because of the treatment they receive, Nobodies feel less than human. They are left out of the community, are non-entities, less than zero. You know when you are treated as a Nobody because you have an empty place right in the middle of your chest where you heart should be.

*The Snob.* Each Aesop fable teaches a lesson. For example, there was a frog who wanted to be as big as an ox. He and all his cousins regularly blew themselves up bigger because the trick elicited a frenzy of enthusiasm from the girl frogs.

Therefore, the frog blew himself up until he was the largest frog on the pond. He continued to blow himself up larger and larger until he burst like a balloon. It is easy to feel satisfaction when we visualize a snob exploding. Rather than sinking to such rankism, how about if we try to better understand snobs.

Joseph Epstein thinks snobbery is a way some people make themselves superior at the expense of others. That sounds like rankism to me. The snob calculates what society considers important. In the United States, individuals indicate their importance by consumer-driven items, such as clothing brands, automobiles, one's school, or occupation. The snob wants to "impress his betters or depress those he takes to be his inferiors, and sometimes both."[4]

Snobs believe others will like them more because of what they own, who and what they know, or how they spend their time. According to Alian DeButton, snobs judge other human beings by only one or two areas, such as income or place of work.[5]

To think about snobs trying to be something they are not helps us revise our initial reaction. Of course, to be profaned by a snob is painful. We may accept the limited perspective of the snob. We may actually suspect we are nothing more than our choice of music or the food we eat.

To understand rankism we need to know how Somebodies misuse their power and how Nobodies respond to mistreatment. The easiest thing is to point our index finger at someone else we call rankist. The difficult part is to accept that we each have been responsible for putting down someone else. Unless we accept that we are more than targets of abuse, that we are also perpetrators in this complicated social interaction, we have no way to improve our lives. When we understand why humans behave as rankists and what techniques Somebodies and Nobodies use against one another, we will be ready to stop cycles of destructive rankist behavior and to reach right-rank.

### Battles among Us

*Conflict happens.* Whether open or opaque, every social hierarchy offers Somebodies control over others. For most of us, there are times when we are satisfied to be helpful and supportive without being in charge. In fact, there are numerous reasons for not accepting leadership roles. Being in charge requires more commitment, more energy, and more work. There are times you may feel it is not important to give so much of yourself. You have other significant things to do.

We may also find our position unsatisfying, maybe not challenging enough, or giving us less to do than we want. If we start searching for ways to challenge the Somebodies, or our place in the hierarchy, that is when conflict becomes inevitable. You voice disagreement with Somebody's decision. If Somebody does not like challenge, conflict happens. If a Nobody employs more subtle means to make a point, conflict happens. Social conflict is part of social hierarchies.[6]

This book does not aim to eliminate conflict from your life. In fact, there are times when you may choose to screw up your courage and make conflict happen. The trick is to have careful plans, remember what you are fighting for, and avoid becoming a rankist during the battle.

*Useful conflict.* Woody loved his job at an independent bookstore. For three years, he listened without comment at department meetings and then followed orders. He never disagreed with the owner until she proposed rearranging the store aisles. The owner planned to increase products by adding more shelves and moving the checkout counter closer to the backroom. This time, Woody spoke up. Weren't customers accustomed to checking out as they left the store? The owner asked what others thought about Woody's comment and a month-long discussion commenced. In the end, a group of employees helped the owner revise the entire store setup, which included more shelf space, more reading space—and checkout up front.

What did Woody do right? First, he knew his boss well enough to know that his question would not intimidate her. Second, he stuck to the issue, revising the store setup. Imagine Woody saying, "Only an idiot would put the checkout at the back of the store!" He would have faced a surprised and likely hostile owner. His fellow workers would have jumped to her defense, and the issue would have been lost.

Taking a chance on conflict can prevent problems in business as well as in the larger world. According to one expert, the attack on Pearl Harbor in 1941 could have been averted had someone pressed the point. Accurate military intelligence was available to the Pacific Fleet Commanders.[7] Some say that if the FBI agents in Arizona and Minnesota had pressed the leadership about terrorist suspects taking flight training, the 9/11 attacks on New York and Washington, D.C., may have been averted.

Conflict can be productive when it peaks the interest of others. Involved members in a group disagreement have greater commitment to the outcome. If you want to move up in a hierarchy, here is one rule to remember: When you speak up and contribute, you get noticed, and you improve your chances of raising your rank.

In democracies, mechanisms for expressing discontent with government are necessary. Conflict is useful when it centers on, for example, laws that seem unfair to a segment of society. The same is true for the delicate balance among parents and children. Teenagers who want to contest rules because they think they are now ready for more freedom need ways to make their views heard. Business also needs mechanisms for dealing with conflict. When a group of employees takes exception to the way promotions are decided, or to any other procedure, they need ways to express their discontent in a civil fashion. The absence of such vehicles of expression can increase the chances of rankism.

*Rankism battles.* A second-year cadet at the U.S. Air Force Academy told a freshman he planned to report her illegal compact disc to academy officials. While this seemed a small offense, she was terrified the academy would toss her out. Her fear turned to panic when the accusing cadet suggested he would forget the violation—if she performed oral sex on him.[8] Investigators found this woman to be one of many female cadets subjected to rankism battles at the Academy.

Conflicts within a hierarchy turn to rankism when someone moves, not to improve things, but to promote personal interests at others' expense. The perpetrator is not interested in what is best for the relationship, the organization, or the community. *Rankism is promotion of oneself and one's interests while bringing harm to a person and/or community.* Unlike useful conflicts that are presented with respect for all and that concentrate on the substance of issues, rankism battles are emotional. People get riled up because they do not feel heard or because they feel demeaned. All parties lose track of where they do and do not agree on the issues because they are battling for recognition and respect.

Not all Alphas (Somebodies) and not all Omegas (even not all Nobodies) abuse rank all the time. Because those who have misused their position have injured us, we may forget that respectful, competent leaders abound. If you do not know Omegas who are models of how to participate in ending rankism, you will meet some later in the book.

When Somebodies work to keep others down, when Nobodies aim to harm those above and tear down the organization that everyone depends on, rankism happens. Once begun, rankism goes on and on.

## Cycles of Rankism

With guidance from her family counselor, Jean began to talk about the situation at work. Until now, Jean had always been a happy person who was proud she could have both a family and a career. She received several promotions and looked forward to her time at work.

Then, a new boss was hired, a boss who criticized everything Jean did. Several times an hour, he would circle her desk, pick up documents she was working on, and loudly point out errors so everyone could hear. Over the last month, Jean had stopped taking a lunch break, could not sleep at night and had intense headaches. She was ashamed to talk to anyone about her continual and mounting mistakes. Therefore, Jean took out her frustration where she knew there would be no reprisals, where she had the power to vent her anger. At home, she yelled and belittled the people she loved the most. Jean had become an abused Nobody Rankist, as well as a Somebody Rankist.

*Both Somebody and Nobody Rankists.* It is comfortable to concentrate on Somebody Rankists. Jean's boss was clearly misusing his position to humiliate her. Are the Somebody Rankists the problem? Only in part. Since we move from hierarchy to hierarchy, we can take out our frustrations on those below us elsewhere.

Some rankists are not at the top or bottom of the hierarchy. They may be in the middle somewhere or further down the line. When we attack those above us in the hierarchy, we become rankists who feel like Nobodies stuck without power to make a change.

We may not act as rankists everyday, but there are times when each of us sits somewhere on the full spectrum of rank abusers. Sometimes, we are rankists when we least recognize it.

*Don't get mad—get even.* Stan had a simple philosophy toward anyone who might intimidate him or his family. "Don't get mad," he would say, "Get even!" In most ways, Stan was a good worker and a good neighbor. When he first espoused his stand against anyone who crossed him, others laughed. Stan let them know he was not kidding. The story he told me concerned his slicing the tires of a car mechanic who overcharged him.

Although he was close to his family, Stan had no friends. His coworkers told me they were wary of him. Moreover, when anything unusual happened, people suspected it was Stan's handiwork. This was a man who had no idea he was a rankist who was perpetuating a cycle of rankism.

*We cheer for rankists.* In the 1990 film *A Shock to the System*, actor Michael Caine played ad executive Graham Marshal. When the main character loses a long-awaited promotion to a younger man, he decides to kill off his competitor, as well as his wife. Marshall gets away with the murders, and decides to take over the company. It is a dark comedy and Caine's acting is outstanding. Audiences cheer the killer, who is a Nobody Rankist of the worst sort and becomes a most despicable Somebody Rankist.

We identify with Nobodies who want to get back at Somebody Rankists. We have all felt slighted at one time or another, and may even have contemplated a plan of our own. When we laugh and cheer a rankist like the Caine character, it may be that we forget the real-life implications.

When researchers looked at school bullies and their targets, they found that both shared many of the same problems. In twenty-five countries, investigators compared over 110,000 eleven- to fifteen-year-olds who were bullies or the bullied to those students who were not involved in bullying. Both bullies and the bullied had more health problems, poorer school adjustment, poorer relations with classmates, and greater use of alcohol.[9] In our real lives, both Somebody Rankists and Nobody Rankists suffer whether they are dispensers or recipients of abuse.

A 2005 survey of college undergraduates found that sixty-two percent, both male and female, experienced sexual harassment in all parts of campus at both public and private institutions. This translates to about six million students. More surprising, fifty-one percent of males and thirty-one percent of females admitted they had sexually harassed others. The reason they gave was "I thought it was funny."[10] People of all ages are unaware of their own rankism.

### Group against Group

The history of humankind is filled with examples of class struggles. We know how the Roman emperors kept their subjects in poverty. We have heard of the old caste system of India wherein each group was encouraged to stay within a closed community for life. Landowners, merchants, artisans, and farmers were spread along a complicated hierarchy. Castes vied for superiority among themselves, but they all agreed that Brahmans (the priests) were the highest, and outcasts (the untouchables) were the lowest. Each caste took care of its own and thought, for one reason or another, that it was superior to other castes. Everyone thought themselves above the untouchables, who are protected by law today. A friend of mine, born in India, married above his caste. He told me that lower caste members rank higher when they acquire education or use their wits to become rich. That is what he did.

*Rankism—"The Mother of All Isms."* Too often, majority groups discriminate against other groups because of their different race, sex, creed, sex/gender orientation, religion, cultural background, or whatever. Robert W. Fuller pointed out that all examples of discrimination share one tactic, to humiliate and demean others. He called rankism the "Mother of All Isms."[11] Discrimination has less to do with the reason—be it political party, religion, or whatever—than with exploiting one group's dominant position. Another author maintained that discrimination of one group against another occurs in all societies in order to maintain that group's social dominance.[12] The teenagers who went online to discredit their teachers and classmates talked about "ranking on someone." It means putting another down, lowering that person's rank so as to elevate one's own.

Variations among groups are carefully manufactured to suit the dominant group. According to Joseph L. Graves, an evolutionary biologist, there is no definitive genetic or observational means to determine racial differences. Humans share 99.8 percent common genes, and race is a socially constructed idea used to keep down certain groups of people. The myth of race, as well as any other manufactured differences, is a type of rankism.[13]

*Institutionalized rankism.* When a dominant group uses hierarchical structures to keep down other groups, rankism becomes officially sanctioned. People accept a corporate culture that hires no Muslims. Slavery was part of American society for so long because no one questioned the laws. The years of racism that followed were still filled with rankism. As Harper Lee showed in *To Kill a Mockingbird*, otherwise good White people assumed that Negroes were lesser beings not worthy of equal treatment. Despite twentieth century labor movements, some companies are still lax about employee safety and benefits. In parts of the world, women are still considered property of their husbands. Rankism is still successfully institutionalized.

Some institutionalized rankism we accept as business as usual. Frank and Cook, authors of *The Winner-Take-All Society*, described how special interest groups seek laws that cut down competition. Even professional associations set hurdles, beyond proof of competence, just to ensure their own monopoly.[14]

*Rankism and violence.* Rankism battles hurt more than those involved in a single altercation because rankism breeds violence. Rollo May, who was interested in the relationship between violence and powerlessness, wrote, "Violence arises not out of superfluity of power but out of powerlessness."[15] From this perspective, we can understand incidents such as school shootings, or that awful term "going postal" as coming from a Nobody Rankist. Violence can come from Nobodies who aim not at just the offending Rankist, but at others, as well.

*Rankism and war.* Rankism leads to war. The American Civil War was about the rankism of slavery. World War II was about Nazi superiority over what they considered lesser countries and lesser peoples, the Jews. In 1983, terrorist suicide bombers attacked the American Embassy in Beirut. In 2001, al-Qaeda members flew airlines into the World Trade Center and the Pentagon. Violence is now the political vehicle of terrorists who have felt like Nobodies. Thus, they become Nobody Rankists and thousands are drawn into wars where they kill and maim—and are killed and maimed.

This book concentrates on rankism in your daily life, those abuses of rank that occur in relationships, families, schools, workplaces, and communities. Yet, we need to be aware that serious worldwide rankism can affect us personally, and that the dynamics of rankism are the same everywhere.

## Chapter Summary

We have begun a journey to right-rank, where everyone treats everyone else with respect and dignity. We looked at our animal friends to learn about how they form hierarchies. With that background, we began to see how human hierarchies are more complicated. We have some hierarchies that are open, even charted, and others that are opaque (more subtle and difficult to grasp). As we move through each day, we humans enter different systems of hierarchy and our standing or rank within those hierarchies moves up and down. We are sometimes thrust into a different rank, and sometimes we carefully plan for a change. Within our hierarchies, Somebodies are given respect, and the power from others to make changes; Nobodies feel they are dehumanized because they receive no encouragement or opportunity for change. When we come together in groups, humans must face conflict, and while some conflicts are useful, others are destructive, rankist battles.

Hierarchies are not responsible for rankist battles. Rankist battles are created by Somebodies and Nobodies who abuse their position within a hierarchy. Learning to take responsibility for our own parts in rankist battles is an important step toward achieving right-rank and stopping the cycle of rankism. Whether a battle starts with one person or within one organization, rankism can lead to battles between groups. Rankism breeds violence, and rankism causes wars. The goal here will be for you to reach right-rank, and use your own position so that everyone is treated decently.

## Reaching for Right-Rank: The Hierarchies in Your Life

Within each social setting, we are part of a different hierarchy. You can write down your answers to these questions on a separate paper or just think about them—whatever works for you.

1.  Choose a day, maybe in the last week. How many social groups were you in? From your perspective, what is the rank order of the members of your group, and what is your rank within that order? How well did members get along with one another? Did they accomplish their goals?

2. What are two situations in which you are a Somebody? Is your position formal (president, chairperson, director) or informal (no title, but others look to your leadership)? How do others treat you when you are the leader? How comfortable are you as leader? Have you ever been disrespectful of anyone when you are leading?

3. Identify two situations where you function under someone else's leadership. Find one leader you have dealt with who you consider competent and considerate of others. Find another who mistreated you or another person. How did you feel about such abuse?

4. Recall a time, maybe now, when you anticipate a change in position within any hierarchy. Have you begun a plan to make the change? Have you let others know you are in charge? Are you going to wait longer before you share your plans?

CHAPTER TWO

# *Notable Hierarchies Include Right-Rank*

**P**eople can make notable hierarchies. We can decide to use our ranking systems for the betterment of all. To create such social mechanisms, we need to know (a) what does and does not work in ridding ourselves of rankism, (b) what a notable hierarchy looks like, and (c) what kinds of rank occur in a notable hierarchy.

### What Does Not Work

*Can not kill all rankists.* I return to our animal friends for another lesson. Alpha baboon males are known for their fiercely intimidating aggression toward females and lower-rank males. When the dominant males of a savanna baboon troop in Kenya all died from contaminated meat, the lower-rank males, who were unwilling to fight for food at the garbage pit, were left with the troop's females and babies. Twenty years after the death of the Alpha males, researchers found the culture of that troop differed from the way it once was, and from any other observed group of wild baboons.

The social climate was now a "relaxed' dominance hierarchy." Lower-rank males, no longer harassed by the more dominant males, were uncharacteristically healthy and unstressed. There was more grooming between males and females and the dominant males moved in closer proximity to other troop members. Because young baboon males leave the family when they are adolescents, within ten years, all males from that original troop were gone. The young males that joined the troop had adapted to the new culture.[1]

So, we suspect that rankism is learned, and hierarchies can change. Could it be that the best way to deal with rank abuse is to kill off all offenders? That right-rank can be achieved only when the abusers are gone and we start anew to create a world where individual dignity is the norm? Probably not. To transfer the wild baboon story to human culture, nothing short of an unforeseen event that killed Somebody Rankists would work. As soon as any human or group of humans sets out to do in rank abusers, they have become rankists. It would be akin to—what should we call it—"abusercide." Moreover, the perpetrators would continue the culture of abuse.

There are other suggestions about dealing with rank abuse. Some suggestions I set out in this chapter make more sense than others. Let us sift through them.

*Can not eradicate hierarchies.* One suggestion for dealing with rankists is to do away with hierarchies. Anarchists detest hierarchies. It is because of ranking systems, they say, that some individuals and some groups dominate and exploit others. Anarchists seek economic, social, and government systems where everyone is equal. It is an interesting theory based on a somewhat convincing concept, but one that has never worked. When those in power abuse the masses, anarchists are available to overthrow the powerful. Whether it is within labor union strikes or government insurrection, anarchists join the fight against authority.

Anarchists have been part of major political revolutions in at least two countries. They joined the Bolsheviks during the October 1917 Russian Revolution only to have their party locked out by the Bolsheviks, who became increasingly more dictatorial and totalitarian.[2]

The Spanish Anarchist Movement of the 1930s created the Spanish National Confederation of Labor, where worker groups formed with no hierarchy. The workers took the factories from the owners and, ran them awhile. Alas, the armies of Franco's fascist government soundly crushed the anarchists and returned the factories to the original owners. Workers meekly returned to their jobs.[3]

The problem with anarchists is they never constitute themselves sufficiently to carry on after the initial mayhem. While the anarchists scramble to make everyone equal, rankists quietly arrange themselves into brigades. These organized rankists then move in and suppress the populace worse than before. Thus, anarchy never lasts long.

*Can not everyone always be equal.* Yes, Thomas Jefferson told us, "All Men are Created Equal." By that we understand that we all, despite our individual differences, deserve equal justice in a court of law. Difficult as equality under the law may be, no one in the United States argues Jefferson's point. The anarchist's dream of a society where everyone is equal in everything does not work. We do not ask a composer of symphonies to fix our roof, or a farmer to remove an appendix.

We each are Somebodies within our realm of influence and something much less in other areas.

*Can not please everyone.* A world where everyone within every hierarchy is treated with dignity will not mean that everyone is always happy. Sometimes, we cannot have what we want. Family members complain that we spend too much time at work. Our favored political candidate loses. The job for which we applied goes to someone else. Notable hierarchies will not make blissfully happy folks of us and will not eliminate disappointment.

Just because we disagree with the way our boss does things does not mean that he or she is a rankist. When your partner offers constructive criticism, it does not mean that you live with a rankist. If parents insist that teenagers do what they ask them to do, it does not mean that the parents are rankists. To call someone a "rankist" just because you disagree with him or her is an act of rankism in itself. Let me say that again. To call others "rankist" when their opinions or actions make you uncomfortable is an act of rankism.

*Can not reach some rankists.* Jacques, a chef for fine restaurants, was notorious for screaming at both kitchen workers and wait staff in the dining room. Occasionally, restaurant guests witnessed his tirades. The owner, who valued Jacques' expertise, spoke to him several times. He needed to change his behavior toward coworkers. When Jacques did not change, he was fired. The owner told me Jacques lost several other jobs because he refused to reign in his outbursts. Jacques probably would not read this book because he has no intention of looking at his own rankism. If he were to, he would recognize himself in Chapter Six as an example of the Seething Giant.

## What Notable Hierarchies Offer Us

While some actions against rankism do not work, notable hierarchies are worth keeping. They offer us invaluable gifts, and notable hierarchies can happen.

*A way of living peacefully.* Organizing by rank helps us to live together peacefully. The failure of anarchists underlines the importance of organizing by rank. Whenever peace is disrupted and a vacuum of power occurs, those who seek control gravitate to positions of command. If there is no system by which rank positions are filled, fights ensue and violence escalates. I am not saying there is never reason to fight, or that some battles are less than commendable. Rather, when we resort to mayhem, we may harm the system and those involved, and we may not successfully end the rankism we deplore. More often, a more successful way is to rework the hierarchy so members are more peaceful.

*Increased productivity.* The second advantage to systems of rank is increased productivity. Look again at the critics of hierarchies. Anarchists espouse decisions by consensus. If one person disagrees, no action is taken. Consensus is important for members of The Friends, also known as Quakers. Quakers are dedicated to peace, so they accept that decisions and actions come slowly.

Within smaller social and business groups, if the stakes are high, consensus within direct democracies is sometimes appropriate. On the other hand, for efficiency and productivity, consensus is too cumbersome. Is it possible for three hundred and fifty million Americans to have a say about everything the federal government does? We can barely achieve a majority to elect a President.

What are the chances we could build a car if every designer and every market person and every line person had a say about window shape and bumper style? The rank system of an automobile manufacturer exists to design, build, and sell cars. Though not perfect, it works well.

Even in our personal lives, rank increases productivity. Imagine preparing for a party and engaging in a lengthy discussion with your fellow organizers about what color napkins to use. Next comes another discussion about which fresh vegetables to offer with which dips. When would you lose patience? Select an Alpha caterer and those details are decided for you. If it is your party, you certainly want to be the Alpha list-maker and, perhaps, the Alpha facility manager.

*Promotion of right-rank.* Exploitation and domination, the problems anarchists criticize about hierarchies, are not inherent to systems of rank. Rather, the perversions they mention come from individuals. It is not the hierarchy that needs to be replaced, but the behavior of individuals who abuse their rank.

Why did factory workers rise up against nineteenth and twentieth century industrialists? Because their safety was ignored, their contributions were presumed, and their compensation was paltry. Why did the Russian people revolt? Because the Tsar was ruthless and unfair.

For democratic citizens, family members, company workers at all levels, there are common goals. We want our organizations to function well. There are ways to reorganize a hierarchy when people disagree with who gives orders, who takes credit, what rewards go to whom. In other words, when there is disagreement over issues of control. In a notable hierarchy, we need not fear conflict because members know they have a chance at fairness.

We can identify and remove rankism without tossing out rank systems that serve us well. To reach right-rank, we need to recognize what different kinds of rank we are dealing with.

## Kinds of Rank

The standing we have within a hierarchy goes beyond a stepladder difference among members. Four types of rank distinctions include positional power, status, fame, and right-rank.

*Positional power.* When a police officer pulls us over in our automobile, we do what we are told. We stay seated behind the wheel and hand our drivers license through the window to the patrolman. When people ask us questions, we answer them. We accept an officer's power because we understand how law enforcement works. If a security guard wants to look in our purse, we allow them to search because we understand it is part of their job. We give positional power to many individuals because of their occupation. Many wear uniforms.

Besides occupation, we also give positional power to some because of their title. Bill Cosby is a comedian, but he is also a doctor of education. When Dr. Cosby talks about education in the black community, he has positional power. Besides occupation and title, we give positional power to some because of their social standing. Higher income is a pretty sure avenue to higher social standing. People listen to Bill Gates not only because he is a business whiz, but because he is one of the richest men in the world.

Positional power allows one to exercise legitimate leadership that can help the entire group to function better. Those who have high positional power offer groups their greater commitment. In turn, they may reap such rewards as personal satisfaction, the appreciation of others, and a positive self-image.

Positional power does not, however, always ensure that the holder will work for a group's betterment. Sometimes, other rewards become selfish reasons for holding positional power. When an elected official holds office, he or she has more opportunity to associate with others who have more money and more power. When politicians with positional power use such opportunities to promote or enrich themselves, rather than the people who elected them, they abuse their rank.

*Status.* The words "rank" and "status" do not mean the same thing. It is worthwhile to see how the words offer us different looks at rankism. Rank has to do with one's level above or below others. Status is the value others attribute to us and our rank. In every community, there are individuals who consider themselves to be the "upper crust." Just because a person has positional power does not mean that he or she has high status. If community members see someone of the "upper crust" as arrogant, selfish, or incompetent, that person's status is low. Status comes from judgments made by others and high status must be earned.

*Fame.* Fame is different from positional power or status. To be famous, all one needs is to be known by masses of people. "Paris Hilton," one commentator said, "is famous for being famous." Fame can bring positional power, and that positional power can be purchased. Fame is often created as part of business with the cooperation of the media.

Fame can be associated with status. Osama bin Laden is famous, but his status is low among Americans. Since he left the White House, Jimmy Carter has continued to be famous. We give him high status, however, because he continues to work tirelessly to promote peace and understanding among often-disparate groups.

Some people who are well known for their high-profile work, artistic achievements, or other well-known contributions try to use their influence in other areas. Sometimes these efforts generate approval or respect and sometimes they do not. Do you ever wonder why a racecar driver or an actor should be considered qualified to advise his or her fans who to vote for? On the other hand, Bono has used his fame to protect the forests and bring attention to AIDS. Two members of the famous Beatles, Paul McCartney and the late George Harrison, both advocated beyond their music for larger world issues. Fame, or celebrity, does not necessarily bring high status anymore than positional power automatically confers high status.

*Right-rank.* Influence that comes from right-rank (treating everyone with dignity, regardless of rank) is associated with status, not fame or positional power. Regardless of our level, we all need to use our position for the betterment of all. It means we demonstrate expertise, wise decision-making and people skills that respect everyone who comes together for a common cause. Right-rank is not just a fanciful idea. It is also practical.

One example of right-rank is a business format, devised by W. Edwards Deming, called Total Quality Management. At each level in a company, small groups, known as Quality Circles, meet to discuss common problems. Not only do workers find problems no one else will recognize, they also create mechanisms for solving the problems. Employees found that with TQM they were treated as more than punch-card workers. Their commitment to the company increased as their contributions were recognized and appreciated.[4]

The difference between abuse of position (rankism) and responsible use of position (right-rank) is sometimes subtle. Here are two examples of sewing teachers, one a rankist, the other of right-rank. The first is a poem.

### Power
*Spiked heels click on hallway tile,*
*purposeful clicking, headed for the Home Economics room.*

*Sewing Machines lined up on one wall face ranges on the other,*
*all waiting to salute her.*

*Flimsy patterns, pinned to printed cotton, lay on tables,*
*tables containing dried bits of farina,*
*left from the morning's experiment.*

*Future homemakers select machines.*
*I choose a corner position*
*away from the center of attention.*

*She visits individual stations,*
*commenting on work in progress.*
*"Nice straight hem, perfect buttonholes."*

*The clicking ceases.*
*Glasses magnifying, peer over my shoulder.*
*"Crooked stitches; rip them out."*

*So went the semester with Miss Sanioca.*
*She, who sewed crooked stitches*
*into my creativity, that took years to rip out,*
*one thread at a time.[5]*

This poem was written by Bobby Walker, finally of retirement age and still bothered by a rankist teacher from her early schooling. Compare Bobby's experience to my own.

My sister and I learned to sew from our mother who was, among other things, an expert seamstress. She took us shopping for material and patterns. Then, she showed us how to carefully cut, sew, fit, resew, and press. I remember her admonition that material cost money, a scarce commodity in our home. Be careful when you cut, she said, because you may not be able to undo a serious mistake. Seams, on the other hand, offer a better chance for correcting errors. No matter how good she may be, sometimes a seamstress has trouble. Be willing, she counseled, to cut and resew a seam. If it works well the first time, great. If not, expect to work until the seam is perfect. For me, these sewing lessons have applied to all other work I have done.

What is the difference between Bobby's teacher and mine? Both meant to educate, but their communication differed. My mother made me feel mistakes were okay and that fixing mistakes was even better. Bobby's teacher just barked her corrections with no concern about how Bobby felt. The message, for Bobby, was she was not good enough. How much better it would have been if Bobby's teacher had let her know she was good enough to be better and not simply robbed Bobby of her dignity.

Wherever we are within a hierarchy, we can best contribute by working for the common goals and treating each person, as well as the full community, respectfully. The Dignitarian Fountain is devoted to protecting the right of everyone to equal dignity, regardless of social position.[6] Right-rank is a challenge directed not just to leaders, but also to each of us to respect one another's humanity.

**Chapter Summary**

There are a number of tactics that will not help us toward right-rank. We cannot kill rankists, or eradicate hierarchies, or make everyone equal at all times, or please everyone. Humans continue to organize into hierarchies because systems of rank help them live peacefully, work together productively, and promote right-rank. Rank includes positional power, which comes from occupations, titles, and money. Rank also includes status, which puts a value on our rank. Fame is a type of rank that makes Somebodies of those known by lots of people. Fame can be earned or purchased, and it may or may not be associated with status. Right-rank is part of status in that how we treat others influences how we are valued. People judge us according to how well we exercise responsibilities of our rank, how well we make decisions, and how well we treat others.

**Reaching for Right-Rank: Somebodies and Nobodies You Know**

1.  Name a Somebody with positional power who also has status (valued for expertise and decision-making). Name a person who demonstrates right-rank (respects

all others). How is that person a Somebody? Name a person in a lower position who garners both status and right-rank.

2. Describe a notable hierarchy of which you are part, where you and others are comfortable, productive, and treated respectfully by all.

3. What examples do you have from your life of those who misuse their position, both Somebodies and Nobodies? Try to be specific. What makes these individuals rankists?

4. Ralph Nader, presidential candidate, said, "There is no left or right. There is only up and down." What was he saying about positional power? Do you think he could be referring to rankism? If so, explain how.

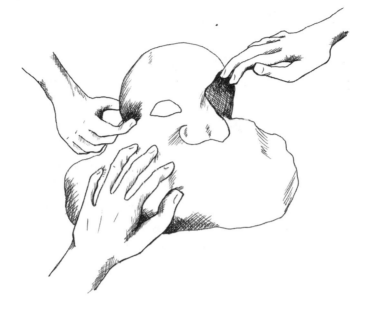

## Part Two

# Rankists Are Made, Not Born

The world cannot be separated into rankists who do evil and the good guys who are put upon by them. Rather, rankists are created. Some rankists are more abusive than most, but we all hold the potential because we are all social beings.

*Social imperative.* Some of us may be more social than others, but we all depend on society to make us human. It is a long and intricate effort to make a fully functioning human being of an infant baby. Our social imperative is part of the reason we are susceptible to rankism. Otherwise, we could do without those who put us down.

*Competition.* We need to find some place where we can push ourselves to excel. Competition can be an important way to stop rankism because the better we do, the greater our opportunities to treat others well. Part of accepting higher positions is accepting the responsibilities that go with them. This can be an exhilarating endeavor.

*Superior and inferior.* As we compete, we need to understand that everyone sometimes wins and sometimes loses. At one time or another, we all feel both superior and inferior. Rankists are unwilling to accept powerlessness, so they do everything to keep themselves superior.

*Fear.* We are wired to notice potential harm. That feeling of fear is innate. We also learn to fear things that pose no immediate danger. Because our fears can be unrealistic, we may be willing to accept rankism. Rankists are very adept at manipulating Nobodies with fear.

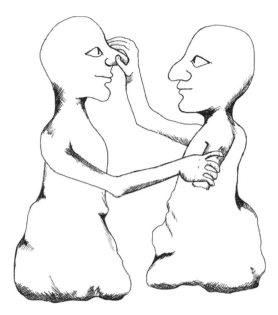

## CHAPTER THREE

# *Humanizing: We Create One Another*

John Donne's phrase "No man is an island, entire of itself,"[1] refers to our need for other humans. We are not born fully human. Rather, we evolve into social creatures by interacting with other humans. Part of the reason rankism is so painful is that people need people. We take for granted our regular interaction with others, and we suffer deeply when deprived of it.

## To Prosper, We Need Other Humans

Within hours of birth, the Caribou calf can walk well enough to follow its mother into the wilds. Human infants take ten to twelve months to walk and twenty years to mature into adulthood. Besides our prolonged physical and mental development, we must learn complex information and skills necessary to function in society. Such accomplishments require intense interaction with other people. When we consider children with limited human contact and adults kept in isolation, we appreciate the importance of human association.

*Feral children.* Youngsters kept in solitude, or who lived alone in the wild before being reintroduced to human community, are known as feral children. One recent story is of a girl called Genie, whom authorities rescued in 1970 from the home of her Los Angeles parents. Genie, who was thirteen, had been kept in a room tied to a potty chair—both day and night—until she was found. When she was discovered, she was the size of a six-year-old and did not speak. With language tutoring, she eagerly began to develop an English vocabulary, but then her progress stopped. Genie was always difficult to understand and she never learned to speak full sentences. Efforts to assist Genie to enter into human-like relationships brought limited success. Added to this, Genie required fulltime care, beyond what most individuals could offer. Thus, she was moved from home to home. Sometimes, her foster parents treated her with affection and patience, but sometimes caretakers were not adept at meeting her needs. At last report, Genie lived in a home for retarded adults.

Another feral child is Cau Cau, an undersized twelve-year-old Chilean boy who had lived in a forest.[2] He had been in the forest for three or more years, having left home during a traumatic family event. After he was brought back to the village, Cau Cau, who preferred to walk on all fours, learned basic vocabulary and could draw well. According to his foster mother, he blushed when he saw a photo of himself naked, but was unable to establish close ties with anyone. He never inquired about other humans, but was attached to his clothes and small animals. Cau Cau could not learn social rules, such as not spitting or urinating anywhere he chose, or touching the breasts of girls he saw. His foster mother said he had "no clear sense of his place in the world." The last news of Cau Cau was that he lived with family members on a farm.

Children without human interaction in their early years never learn thinking language and the nuances of social living. So far as we know, they never will be able to live independently in our human world.

*Solitary confinement.* Another way to appreciate the importance of human contact is to realize the effects of solitary confinement. To punish or control them, prison administrators sometimes put inmates by themselves, even away from sound, sight, and odor stimuli. The writer, James Fennimore Cooper, wrote:

> Of all the ingenious modes of torture that have ever been invented, that of solitary confinement is the most cruel—with the mind feeding on itself with the rapacity of a cormorant.[3]

Stuart Grassian found that the effects of solitary confinement among convicts in Massachusetts were akin to those that American prisoners reported during the Korean War. The isolated men developed extreme sensitivity to external stimuli, such as sounds and smells. They found themselves unable to distinguish reality from imagination, such as: did the guard threaten the prisoner or did he imagine it. They experienced sudden anxiety attacks with increased heartbeat, shortness of breath, dizziness, and headaches. They also were troubled by persistent dreams of violence against the guards. When reintroduced to the general population, some men managed to recover well enough, whereas others continued to have psychological problems.[4]

The affects of confinement afflicted members of Biosphere, an experiment that placed people, plants, and animals within a closed physical environment. In a large glass enclosure situated in the Arizona desert, eight people spent two years isolated from the rest of the world. They had physical problems because the plants did not produce sufficient oxygen, so they piped air in. Equally important, they lacked a sufficient number of people to enrich their lives. Communication became a serious problem among members. By the sixth month they had divided into two factions of four. Groups refused to speak to one another. One member described the problem as "impression starvation." The lack of various friends and interesting new people weighed heavily on their ability to function.[5]

Our extraordinary reaction to the loss of human contact has to do with our basic need for human communication—as basic as eating and sleeping. Communication is the way we know who we are and how to function among our fellow humans.

### We Owe It All to Others

To understand why rankism is so harmful, we need to know how we become social beings. George Herbert Mead (1867–1931) thought a lot about this question.[6] He contended that we become fully human only through communication with other humans. We are born with but the potential, and we learn to become human by creating a sense of "Self." To do that, we must be part of a community. We owe who we are to other people, some of whom may treat us as Somebodies and some of whom may treat us as Nobodies.

*Our self.* When we talk about our "self," we first think of an object. That is how our sense of self begins. At a young age, we notice our bodies and compare them with others' bodies. Here is an easy quiz. Given the options, is your

- body tall or short, thin or thick, muscular or soft?

- skin yellow or pink or brown or black, light or medium or dark, smooth or rugged, clear or marked, taut or relaxed?
- hair curly or straight, heavy or thin, coarse or smooth, black or brown, or blond or red?
- eye shape almond or slanted up or slanted down, colored blue or brown or black or hazel or green or gray?
- nose long or short, straight or curved, broad or thin?

Are your

- hands long or short, wide or narrow?
- feet long and wide, arches high or low, toes long or short?
- nails thick or thin?

For you and me, answers to these questions take no effort. Not so for feral children. They never learned to compare their bodies with those of others. You and I have a good sense of where our skin stops and where the cool (or warm) air begins. Feral children lack the sense that this is their body; rather they seem not to notice when their bodies are injured, cold, or ill.

*Our talents.* When the girl was seven years old, her mother bought an old upright piano because the child said she wanted to play. The lessons in the second-story room of an old Victorian house were magical. Mrs. Wilson, her piano teacher, was beautiful, and the essence of wild roses surrounded the girl as they sat together on the piano bench. At the end of the lesson, Mrs. Wilson would play the pieces for the following week. Without that, the girl would have been lost, because she could not read music very well. The girl talked a lot about her piano lessons and practiced seldom.

One afternoon, with the big family gathered at Grampa Mike's, the little girl was invited to play for everyone. While confident when she sat at the piano, the girl could barely stumble through "Humoresque." I was that child. At a tender age, I realized that neither Mrs. Wilson playing the song nor my talking about lessons could define me as a piano player. I decided to quit pretending I wanted to pay the price to learn.

Everyone is good at something, and nobody is good at everything. Of all the amazing things some individuals can do, how do we learn what are our special talents?

How did Michael Jordan realize he played basketball so well? How did Jesus, Muhammad, the Buddha, Gandhi, and Mother Theresa learn their special talents were spiritual. How did Marie Curie, who discovered radium, realize she was good at science? They learned about their talents from those around them. So do we all. People caught in the cycle of rankism may not learn what they do well.

Besides recognizing our gifts, we must figure out what are our likes and dislikes. We tend to develop those talents that delight us and avoid those we abhor. Our goals grow out of our talents, interests, and likes.

Kevin was a talented mathematician who received a full scholarship to one of the best universities. There he achieved the highest math scores in the school's history. Professors were enthused about Kevin's potential and had a variety of ideas of how he could best use his extraordinary talent. The young student found math easy—and boring. In his freshman year, Kevin received all A's, except one C in sociology. You guessed it. The teenager decided to pursue a degree in sociology—a field in which he eventually excelled. How lucky for Kevin that his parents let him find his own way. In a cycle of rankism, Kevin might have stayed where he was unhappy and never pursued his dreams.

*Our feelings.* After her divorce, JoAnne wanted to know why her marriage had been so difficult for her. She continued to see her counselor and began to read and take courses.

JoAnne told me she learned that as a child her emotions had been denied. When she was angry, her mother told her she was mean. When she was sad, her mother called JoAnne whimpy. Only when she was happy did her mother agree JoAnne was happy.

Throughout her marriage, JoAnne was never sure how she felt when her husband kept changing jobs and expecting her to pack up, leave her friends and her job. Through eight relocations in five years, JoAnne kept stuffing her emotions until one day she began to cry and could not stop. JoAnne said what she learned was, "My feelings are me. Good or bad, I have a right to experience my emotions."

Our emotions are the energy that comes from being part of life. If others ignore or misrepresent our emotions, we have trouble embracing an important part of who we are. To ignore the feelings of others is a basic way that rankism can cause damage.

*Our community.* Feral children can never be part of a community. For us to participate in a community, we must know who we are, how we feel, and what choices of response are available to us. We need one another to create visual arts and music, as well as families, companies, clubs, schools, religious communities, cities, and nations. Any organization is created and maintained by the contributions of many humans with a sense of Self. Their hierarchies are made possible by communication interaction.

## Empathy

Standing naked before the full-length mirror, he looked at himself head-on. Then, he turned to the right and gazed over his shoulder. He pulled in his stomach and threw out his chest, bent his left arm, and flexed his biceps. After a pause, he moved close to the mirror and studied his face. Indeed, there were stiff hairs poking through his upper lip. He smiled and noticed how his eyes automatically shone. Finally, he donned his most stern frown. He was someone to take seriously. He was going to make a fine impression tonight at the school game. He was looking so good.

When a young man wants to know how he is coming across to others, he does more than look in the mirror. He mentally becomes the audience looking at his image. He jumps into his friends' bodies and minds. He tries to see and feel the world as they do.

Empathy makes possible our sense of oneness with all humanity. As we communicate with others, we understand how they perceive the world. We recognize what it means to be human. We all are sometimes happy and sometimes angry or sad. We all celebrate and grieve. We all are sometimes confident and sometimes unsure.

Empathy helps us understand how a Somebody can become a rankist and how a rankist's target feels like a Nobody.

**Chapter Summary**

Hierarchies that allow rankists to mistreat others are not something far outside us. Rather, we each help create and maintain various human levels. The only way to become social humans is to interact with others. Unlike feral children, who were deprived of humanizing processes, we communicate with others to mutually define one another. Our Self comes, in great part, from those around us. They help us define our talents and interpret our feelings. Together, we build all groups with various hierarchies. When we empathize with others, we become members of the human species. What wondrous and creative beings we are!

**Reaching for Right-Rank: Your Reactions to Rank Conflict**

1.   Who contributed to your sense of Self? Who helped you learn your talents? In your early years, were your feelings acknowledged, or were your emotions redefined? By whom?

2. Take the following self-inventory of your reactions to rank conflict.

## Rank Conflict Inventory

The Rank Conflict Inventory is a tool for understanding rankists and for moving yourself into right-rank. In each grouping, think of ONE SITUATION you have been in. If you wish, select a different situation for each grouping. For example, in section "A" you might select a time you gave a report and someone belittled you. For section "B" you might remember a time you were accused of something you did not do.

If every option in a given group leaves you uncomfortable, join the throng. Most of us are uneasy with some choices. Still, choose TWO (2) numbered responses in each grouping that are most like the way you would respond.

THE EASIEST WAY TO TAKE THIS INVENTORY IS TO WRITE ON A PIECE OF PAPER THE LETTER AND THEN NUMBERS OF THE TWO ITEMS YOU SELECT FROM THAT GROUPING.

A. When my standing is challenged, I
  1. insist that the challengers do things correctly.
  2. yell when someone deserves it.
  3. give it right back to the challengers.
  4. convince the challengers that their treatment of me is wrong.
  5. expect to be paid well for putting up with the challengers' insults.
  6. find ways to help my friends, not the challengers.
  7. strike out at someone else.
  8. know who will keep the challengers in line.
  9. say something nice to the challengers.
  10. rally others against my mistreatment by the challengers.

B. When I am wronged I
   11. take further advantage of all available privileges.
   12. find a way to pay the offender back.
   13. tell others the faults of those who wronged me.
   14. remember who is loyal to me.
   15. try to understand the one who wronged me
   16. press hard for others to get things done on time.
   17. appreciate those who enforce the rules.
   18. get indignant when others miss the mark.
   19. stay peaceful.
   20. ignore the incident.

C. When I am in charge, I
   21. point out who made mistakes.
   22. have no time to learn others' names.
   23. help only those who merit help.
   24. like compliments.
   25. accept no excuses.
   26. deserve thanks for helping others.
   27. set my own hours.
   28. stretch the truth somewhat.
   29. do not hold back on my anger.
   30. have everyone watch for troublemakers.

D. When I am put down unfairly, I
   31. praise the persons.
   32. try to better myself.
   33. bear my burden.
   34. persuade the abusers to stop.
   35. devise a plan to get even with them.
   36. muster others to take a stand against put-downs.
   37. set aside my feelings.
   38. start a rumor about the denigrators.
   39. take it out on another.
   40. put that person down.

E.  When provoked by others, I
41. withhold information from the irritants.
42. badger someone else.
43. press for provokers who messed up to fess up.
44. make sure I am credited for whatever I oversee.
45. work with provokers to change their behavior.
46. do not have time to say hello to everyone.
47. find an organization that will support me against the provokers.
48. aggravate the provokers right back.
49. use the provoker's soft spots to my advantage.
50. give the provokers credit.

F.  When I am treated badly, I
51. find ways to tie those who mistreat me to my control.
52. pass on hearsay about the offenders.
53. surround myself with gifted helpers.
54. swallow the pain.
55. think of other things.
56. stay too busy to socialize.
57. get the bad guys when they do not notice.
58. know who makes me look bad.
59. hope things will improve.
60. block those who hurt me

If you cannot wait to learn how to interpret this inventory, you may refer to the end of Chapter Eight. But if you wait until you have read all the chapters leading up to that point, you will better understand how to use the Rank Conflict Inventory to reach right-rank.

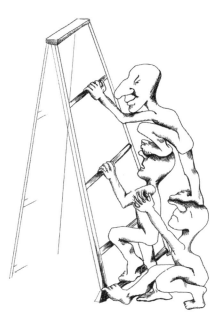

## CHAPTER FOUR

# *Competition:*
# *Capturing a Top Spot*

To stop any instance of rankism, we need to understand the impetus for seeking the highest position. What competitions might you choose to engage in? What would you expect to gain from achieving that particular top spot? To help you answer such questions, we are going to explore some ideas about why humans seek power. The eighteenth-century German philosopher Nietzsche was one of the first to take on the topic. Alfred Adler, an Austrian psychoanalyst and social thinker, offered a different perspective on humans. At the end of the chapter, I will advance some comments on the morals and wisdom of chasing power.

## Which Battle on Which Ladder?

*Do not limit your dreams.* Robert Frank and Philip Cook described how American culture has created an economy based on mega audiences with a few select performers in the top spot. Because it requires less work to deal with only a few high-income commodities, they say, insiders such as producers and marketers prefer systems that keep others out. In our "Winner Take All" society, the likelihood that talented individuals will be able to reach larger audiences decreases.[1]

It is a mistake to suggest that Somebodies are found only among those who compete in these closed hierarchies. Frank and Cook acknowledged the importance of competition. If we were promised good food and comfortable housing without making an effort, few of us would bother to better ourselves. We might never develop our special talents or know the satisfaction of personal accomplishment.

I gained an inkling of the variety of hierarchies in which anyone might compete when I entered the term "Top Spot" into my Internet search engine. Here is a sample of what popped up: "Storage venders vie for top spot," "Three students compete for top spot," "Serena eyes top spot," "Cisco loses top spot in niche cable market," "Kahlon pole-vaults to top spot," "Baylor Law nabs top spot in bar exam pass," "Hewlett-Packard takes top spot in Newmarketing 100."[2]

*Take a chance.* In our lives, we can find all sorts of contests for top spots. I hope you decide to jump into the fray and work your way up the ladder. Choose where to compete and in what realm. Figure out the set of rules for moving up the ladder. Find contests where you can do well—where your talents and passions can blossom. Find a hierarchy where you can make a difference. Run for the city council; enter a Scrabble tournament; join a soccer league; apply for a job you want. Winning is never a sure thing. It is okay to lose because you will probably learn much more than you ever would have known if you had not tried. Losing does not make us Nobodies.

Competition can be exhilarating, and the battle against rankism is not a battle against competition. True, some competition gives an unwarranted edge to Somebodies over Nobodies. When that happens, changes need to be made. Infractions by skating judges in the 2002 Olympics led to a new system of scoring. If contests within a hierarchy are rankist, challenge them.

We cannot learn about rankism and our place within any hierarchy without understanding why we humans want power. Let us look at what a couple of thinkers suggested about power seeking.

## Will to Power

Friedrich Wilhelm Nietzsche, the German philosopher, was interested in humans striving for power. Nietzsche describes what I call the desire to be a Somebody as instinctive. Each human being, he wrote, has

> [a] will to strive to grow, spread, seize, become predominant…because it is living and because life simply is will to power.[3]

We all want a top spot. We learn early where we fit among those around us. We learn who—our parents or teachers or older kids—are stronger than we are. We notice who—younger children or family pets—look up to us and treat us as more important. We test the boundaries of these rankings to see how we can move up. Yet, there are always those individuals who have places above ours.

As teens, we may notice that those with more formal education are speakers at meetings. Musical groups have recordings that large numbers of people hear on radio or at concerts. Certain professionals wear the most fashionable clothes. Athletes make television appearances and are asked their opinions.

We realize that not all people get to a specific top rung, and we study how some of those who did achieve a top spot managed to do it. Did they organize their time every day studying their school lessons, or doing scales on a guitar, or throwing a ball through a hoop? What activities should we concentrate on so we can achieve the highest notch in our chosen area?

*Power and values.* Because we want to be more powerful, wrote Nietzsche, we also choose our values to suit what we think we can accomplish. This is where we begin to grasp differences between Somebodies and Nobodies. In *On the Genealogy of Morals,* Nietzsche wrote about two sets of morals: morality viewed by what he called the "master class" (Somebodies or Alphas of high rank) and those of the "slave class," which we might know as workers (Omegas, or Nobodies down the ladder). The masters, according to Nietzsche, consider power good and themselves the only ones worthy of having power. To reach his or her highest potential, said Nietzsche, a person of power would push, shove, and force in whatever fashion necessary to become predominant. Workers, he wrote, define as good those things that encourage humility and gentleness—character traits usually missing among the masters. Workers also foster the moral right to revenge against the upper class.[4]

Nietzsche's ideas are insightful. We do justify our actions based on whether we consider ourselves Somebodies or Nobodies. Our moral stands shift if we move from Somebodies to Nobodies, or in the other direction.

If I am a department manager in a manufacturing plant, I consider it a moral obligation to get the product out on time—no matter what is required of workers. If I am an elected official who promised to build a bridge, I figure it is fine to do whatever it takes to the get that bridge built. Both the department manager and the politician are approaching life with Somebody morality.

If I work for a manager who keeps changing deadlines, I criticize such heartless behavior and begin to think of ways to get at the manager. If the politician wants me to pay more than my share for the bridge, I raise a ruckus. Whether Alpha or Omega, we take pride in our actions, even if others think us despicable. Nietzsche has a point when he suggests that we view right and wrong from our position of rank.

*Power and rankism.* Nietzsche's philosophy, however, has serious flaws. In later life, he decided a creative genius (a rare individual such as himself) could ignore social rules that stood in the way of gaining power.[5] Nietzsche not only exposed what I call rankism, he sanctioned rankism—at least for "special" individuals. He missed the implications of what separate moral codes do to society when some, who consider themselves above the usual mass of humanity, set out to squash anyone who is not "special." Hitler and the German Nazis used the works of Nietzsche to justify killing millions of Jews. I think it is easy to see how Somebodies would consider Nietzsche's later works reason to declare themselves "special" while feeling free to mistreat regular folks.

Those who use their position of power to injure others are rankist, whether or not they call themselves Nazis. Battles begin when those who are put down decide to rise up and fight back. There is a better view of competition that helps us deal with one another.

## Both Superior and Inferior

Alfred Adler is another who wrote about human behavior and power. He agreed with Nietzsche that we possess "absolute primacy of the will to power."[6] Adler, however, went beyond Nietzsche when he asserted that "to be human means to feel inferior."[7] Nietzsche thought there were innately superior and innately inferior beings, and that we are one or the other. Adler insisted that we all seek power and all feel inferior.

Part of our challenge as humans is to balance our desire for power with our sense of being in less than the top spot. What I call rankist, Adler would explain as neurotic personality traits. For Adler, rankism would be our inability to adapt well to our internal conflict—that is, between our inner Somebody (superior) and our inner Nobody (inferior).

As I interpret Adler, he believed that Somebody Rankist behavior comes from trying to be perfectly superior and "excluding permanent humiliation" from our experience.[8] Somebody Rankists want to be in the top spot at all times, to allow no one to challenge that position. Somebody Rankists imagine themselves always in control with none to demean them. This absolute power they seek is impossible. We all feel strong and powerful sometimes and lowly and powerless at other times. When Somebody Rankists try to create a world where they totally exclude their own inferior self, terrible things happen to those around them.

*Hitler: Nobody turned Somebody Rankist.* When a person who feels inferior becomes powerful, terrible things can happen. Adolf Hitler was one of the most destructive Somebody Rankists of the twentieth century. Young Adolf seems to have failed early in life and was deeply humiliated by numerous rejections in his Nobody position. When he joined a political group, his speaking achievements swept him up the political ladder. As ruler of Germany, Hitler convinced the German people they were better than the rest of the world. It was the right of German people, he proclaimed, to be above all other humans, especially the Jews, whom he designated as Nobodies.[9] As a Somebody Rankist, Hitler considered it acceptable to destroy anyone and anything he chose.

*Nobody student turns rankist.* A young student in Erfurt, Germany, was expelled. On April 27, 2002, he entered his former school and killed seventeen students and teachers. He was so distressed by being tossed out of school that he wanted to punish everyone associated with the institution. He knew these people had assaulted his self-worth and he actually expected to feel elevated when they were dead.[10]

Terrible things also can happen when individuals feel so deprived and so put down that they cannot manage their inferior position. For the Nobody Rankist, it is not enough to advance; rather, anyone with power must be brought down. Because they feel inferior, Nobody Rankists' "goal of superiority is to suppress the other person."[11] If those in power can be harmed, the Nobody Rankist expects to be doubly superior.

*Rankists are immature and selfish.* In his portrait of what I call a rankist, Adler goes beyond a description of one who cannot balance inner struggles between super and inferior. Adler added this description of one who

> ...strives toward personal superiority and, in doing so, expects a contribution from the group in which he lives, while the normal individual strives toward the perfection which benefits all.[12]

Adler was detailing behavior we see in the very young. Small children want everyone to make them the center of the world. With maturity and learning we realize we owe something to the group. I think it helps to understand that rankists act like selfish children who have yet to leave the playground. Adler continued:

> Maladjustment consists essentially of the more "selfish" striving for a goal of personal power and self-enhancement rather than of a more selfless striving

for perfection.... These represent an early extreme lack of satisfaction of the striving for security and self-esteem.[13]

To work for the greater social good is one way to move beyond the battles between Somebodies and Nobodies. Oh my! What a difficult challenge for anyone who feels buoyed by power or angered by suppression. Our knee-jerk reaction is to fight for ourselves—and then the war escalates.

## Power and Duty

When we successfully gain power, we accept our new rank with additional obligations. Anyone who accepts power without taking on the duty to treat everyone with fairness and dignity becomes a rankist. Here are a couple of points about the implications of duty and obligation for reaching right-rank.

*Beware of "evil" labels.* The film *The Killing Fields* concerned the regime of Pol Pot, who was dictator of Cambodia from 1975–1979. He is responsible for the genocide of over a million of his own people. If they were intellectuals or reasonably successful in business, or if he distrusted them, Pol Pot had them tortured and killed. Pol Pot was described as a gentle man of great charm and social grace. One journalist who met him said he would sit motionless as he spoke, "except for an occasion flicking of the wrist."[14]

I know some would like to say that rankists are just evil. That may be so, but I reject use of the label "evil" as a glib comment or as a cop-out for something one merely fears, strongly disagrees with or cannot understand. How many people throw up their hands and declare, "the sexual predator Jeffrey Dahlmer was evil!" "Stalin was evil!" "Hitler was the most evil man of the century." All were Somebody Rankists. All attempted to keep their power position by hurting others. To declare a

Somebody Rankist as evil adds little to our understanding of rankism. That which is evil is way out and away from us, and we plan to keep it there. We can understand rankists without accepting their behavior.

Since our goal is to stop rankism, we need to bring rankists to a closer human level. Claims that rankists are evil just continue the cycle of abuse. If we think rankists are simply evil, we are not inclined to bridge the chasm between perpetrator and target.

It is more productive for us to recognize rankist behavior as neurotic, as maladaptive. Rankists are trying to safeguard their own self-esteem. To feel inferior is terrifying for rankists. They want a system that protects them as they figure out the future.[15] And they do it in a variety of ways.

Adolf Hitler and Pol Pot were both despots and both Somebody Rankists of the worst kind. In some ways, they share characteristics with others we find difficult to understand. Hannah Arendt studied Adolf Eichmann, one of Hitler's henchmen, during his trial. She summarized his behavior as "the banality of evil." She said he did not hate the Jews. He was just doing his job and, in doing so, used no self-reflection or judgment. He never considered the effect of his work on individuals he imprisoned and killed, and had no empathy for their suffering.[16]

Primo Levi, who was in a Nazi camp, considered all those who contributed to the Holocaust. He included those at the top, like Eichmann, who made the decisions, those who ran the camps, and all those who chose to ignore outward signs of required Stars of David, ghettos, and trains. Levi thought those at the top were clearly criminal and that infants who were not yet able to distinguish between right and wrong were definitely not at fault. Everyone else was in a "Gray Zone."[17]

When you think of rankism as ordinary, it becomes less far away than something evil. Rankism becomes something we can fight. Rankists are both ordinary and awful. The feat is for us to recognize rankism. Then, we can do something about it, something more than finger-wagging.

*Wisdom with power.* Thomas Jefferson left us many astute observations, often dressed in beautiful words. One quotation I especially like is, "I hope our wisdom will grow with our power, and teach us, that the less we use our power the greater it will be." As you grow in understanding rankism, I hope you can remember Jefferson. Lou told me about a friend of his. He asked about her new work with added responsibilities. She reported she was still contributing, and she was learning to lead with modesty. Lou's friend sounds like a good Somebody.

One reason for you to seek a top spot is so you can practice right-rank and enrich your own and others' lives.

## Chapter Summary

To fight misuse of power, we need to decide where we are going to seek a top spot. In this chapter, we covered two approaches to humans seeking power. Nietzsche said we all seek power and those who deserve to be on top create a value system that keeps them above others. Alfred Adler thought that all humans both want power and feel inferior. Rather than call rankists "evil," I suggest we listen to Adler, who believed that rankists are people who cannot accommodate their strong and incompatible feelings of superiority and inferiority. It is possible, thought Adler, for each of us to work for the greater social good. I say that is one way to reach right-rank and battle rankism.

There is more to the power battles between Somebodies and Nobodies. The next chapter will delve more deeply into the human psyche to show how fear pushes our warlike rankist behavior.

**Reaching for Right-Rank: When You Are in the Top Spot**

1.  In what arenas would you like to compete? Have you figured out how to make that happen? What concerns you most about taking the chance?
2.  When you are in a Somebody (Alpha) position, how do you take charge? For example, is your voice stronger? Do you look others directly in the eyes? How do others let you know they consider you to be the Somebody, the leader.
3.  How do you let others know you appreciate their work? Do you ever get peeved at those you depend on who do not come through? How do you express your feelings?
4.  When you feel like a Nobody, or inferior, what brings that on? Are you vulnerable to a particular rankist you know?

## CHAPTER FIVE

# Fear: The Emotion That Shoves Us Up—and Sometimes Over

Dorothy Thompson, who was a suffragist and courageous journalist, wrote early on about Adolf Hitler's rise in Germany. Thompson is purported to have written, "The most destructive element in the human mind is fear. Fear creates aggressiveness." Thompson was right. Fear fuels rankism. To reach and maintain right-rank, we need to understand how fear affects our battles between Somebodies and Nobodies First will be a discussion of different kinds of fears. Second are some ideas of how fear is infused into American society and how easily we can overreact. Third, I will share some ways to manage your own fears and acknowledge those of others. All of this is designed to help you reach right-rank.

## Some Different Fears

Some of our fears are attached to real threats, and some come more from our imagination. Both phobias and anxiety are confusions we create for ourselves. Other fears are inflicted on us by those who want to control our behavior. Last, we will look at a special fear, the fear of knowing ourselves.

*Safety alarm.* Fear, like joy, sadness, and anger, is a basic human emotion. When we perceive any threat that might endanger our safety, fear kicks in. Fear is, perhaps, the first emotion we experience (fear of falling). Certain fears seem to be innate. All humans are born with fear reactions to loud noises, to pain, and to physical injury.[1] These are signs that we are physically threatened, and such fears help us survive.[2] There are some genuine dangers we need to be aware of—such as walking onto a freeway or stepping out of a moving automobile. That safety alarm sends out a loud jolt lest we miss the obvious.

With fear comes physical change. Our heart rate increases, our muscles tremble, our breathing becomes faster and shallower, and our sweat pours forth. We may need to be gladiators protecting ourselves, or track stars sprinting toward shelter. From our ancestors, we inherited this unique mechanism that signals us that danger is near.

If the story of fear stopped here, it would be a simple and straightforward tale. Sometimes, we mistake what is and is not a real threat.

*Misplaced phobias.* Thirty-five-year-old Jamie traces his fear of sharks to the 1975 movie *Jaws.* He realizes now that his only likelihood of encountering a shark is to visit an ocean or aquarium. As a child, however, he had nightmares about sharks and lived daily in fear of sharks leaping out to tear away his baby skin.

No one could convince little Jamie that sharks never live in the Southwest desert where he grew up. As he matured, Jamie realized the difference between imagined fears and those based on real threats from the world.

Phobias, such as Jamie's fear of sharks, are fears of specific places or things that present no immediate threat. Phobias can be debilitating, and those suffering from phobias may need a professional to help deal with their fears. Ronald M. Doctor and Ada P. Kahn wrote of numerous kinds of phobias.[3] Some are familiar, such as claustrophobia (fear of confined spaces) or arachnophobia (fear of spiders).

Others phobias Doctor and Kahn mentioned were some we may have experienced, but were unable to name, such as Bogyphobia (fear of a bogeyman) or Testophobia (fear of taking tests), or Glossophobia (fear of public speaking). All of these are fears that many of us have.

The Doctor and Kahn book identifies other, unrealistic fears that tap our imagination. How, we might wonder, could someone acquire such a phobia as Ambulophobia (fear of walking or of riding vehicles), Syngenesophobia (fear of relatives), Photoaugiaphobia (fear of bright lights) or Pentheraphobia (fear of one's mother-in-law)? Because humans have such varied experiences, we can never formulate a full list of phobias.

A proverb says, "A scalded cat dreads cold water." Humans display the same sort of unreasonable thinking. We are baffling in that we connect threats from one part of life to other aspects of our existence, a different place and time. Say a dog bit you, and the experience was both terrifying and painful. It is possible that every time you see any dog, those feelings of terror return. A neighbor's gentle family pet appears to be a vicious wolf. Sometimes, it is difficult to understand why we fear something, or to connect that feeling of dread with some previously terrifying experience. What we need is a sense that our phobias do not make us Nobodies.

*Misplaced anxieties.* The September 11, 2001, attacks on World Trade Center towers and Pentagon affected all Americans. For some, however, it was the beginning of full-blown anxiety. Children, especially, needed adult support to help them regain a sense of security. Even some adults suddenly worried that terrorists were lurking everywhere. Anyone they did not personally know, particularly if they appeared to be of Middle Eastern origin, became suspect.

Anxieties, like phobias, are not based on real threats. Whereas phobias are focused on a fear of some specific aspect of the world, anxiety is a more generalized fear. Like phobias, anxiety is painful and exhausting. If we are anxious, we are afraid and we cannot say why. When we are threatened in a battle between Somebodies and Nobodies, these anxieties circle our lives and complicate an already perplexing situation.

*Feigned fear.* It seems strange, but fear sells. How can that be? If fear means danger, it makes some sense to avoid instances where it signaled we were in peril. Why would we seek occasions that trigger our physical and emotional response to fear?

Consider that we seek—actually enjoy—hearing scary stories. How many kids sit around dark living rooms or smoldering campfires and whisper of things that go bump in the night? Some savor horror films. Stephen King has made a commendable reputation by scaring the wits out of us.

We even stand in line at amusement parks and pay to ride on roller coasters and other rides that will zip, swing, toss, and drop us. Many folks spend their free time subjecting their bodies to ferocious treatment by practicing extreme sports such as bungee-jumping. And they call it entertainment. The rush of fear can be delicious.

What we carry into all these fright-filled frolics is our knowledge that they are not quite real. Scary fables could happen, yet we are tucked away safely away at home. We believe the creators of fast rides are careful to never put us in harm's way. That we are drawn to fear makes us susceptible to rankists who would use fear against us.

## Fear as Battle Weapon

Unlike entertainment from authors, filmmakers, and storytellers who play with our fear, radio, newspapers, and television use fear as a weapon. When those who control media deliberately create fear in us, they do so to control or manipulate us.

Eric Hoffer wrote, "It is when power is wedded to chronic fear that it becomes formidable."[4] I will include lots of detail here because Americans who struggle with rankism live in chronic fear thrust on us by a powerful media. In order to stop rankism in your life, you would do well to be aware of how fear plays a part in nearly all our hierarchies.

*Frightful news for profit.* Anxiety is part of living in these precarious times. We hear that people are being robbed, killed, and falsely imprisoned. We are told of hazards out there we would never, ever, have imagined. It is no wonder we become anxious about threats in our world. Just watch the evening news filled with fires, auto accidents, thefts, unsolved murders, and criminal trials. The media offers us a slant that emphasizes bad news. There are some explanations about why radio, television, and newspapers contribute to our sense of pervading fear.

Above all, media news is a business. As James Hamilton pointed out, readers and viewers are given news so advertisers can sell their products.[5] Stories of conflict laced heavily with fear attract audience attention. (Remember how we are drawn to scary stories and movies?) As recipients of news, we have trouble separating the emotional presentation from the facts of the story. We are confused, according to Bonnie Anderson, because news today has become "infotainment," information presented to entertain rather than to truly inform.[6]

David Altheide described how media presents news as drama that depends on generating fear to achieve its maximum effect.[7] Stories are framed as problems and only news people know the solution to the crises. Complex issues come to us as simple tales, as morality plays. We are told who are good guys and who are bad, who is fearful and who is fearsome. This is power gained through fear. Moreover, we are seldom given a full picture of what is happening.

Because this format is familiar to media audiences, we come to expect ominous news, and we experience fear "across topics." We no longer merely fear crime, but transfer our fear to embrace concerns about child safety, school gangs, drugs, neighborhoods, and immigrants. These news stories tell us who the "others" are. We no longer trust our teachers, law enforcement officers, judges, doctors, salespersons, politicians, or neighbors. We are set up to strike at all those who could possibly harm us. As Altheide put it, "fear is one of the few perspectives that citizens share today."[8] This media-induced fear allows Somebodies to gain greater control of society.

*Crime, crime, and more crime.* While Americans are healthier, safer, and longer-lived than most any group in history, we see ourselves at greater risk.[9] Crime and other threats seem to be everywhere. Media reporters have a device that makes their jobs so much easier—the police scanner. How much more efficient to listen to the police scanner, then follow the patrol cars and ambulances. It is time consuming to dig into events that are more indicative of what is happening in our communities. How often do we hear about Boy Scout outings, or high school teams doing car washes to raise money for new uniforms, or service clubs contributing money to the local library, or marathoners running to collect contributions for cancer or diabetes?

The truth is that the United States has been experiencing a decrease in criminal activity for some time. According to the U. S. Department of Justice, violent crimes in 2002 continued to decline since 1994 to the lowest level ever recorded.[10] Property crimes continued a twenty-year decline.[11] The Federal Bureau of Investigation reported that from 1993 to 2002, the crime index rate fell twenty-five percent.[12] Why are we not told about these numbers? Instead, we are led to believe that the world and our neighborhoods are more dangerous than ever. Again, fear is a weapon of control.

*Effects of TV violence.* When television news relies on stories of crime and dramatically emphasizes fear, our psyches are seriously affected. It was Marshall McLuhan who first described how television is different from other media because we take in TV differently than newspapers or radio.[13] McLuhan described newspapers as "hot," because we perceive violence reported in papers as if it could hurt us. So, we keep fearful events in print distant from our most vulnerable selves. We drop the terrifying facts as if they were served on a hot plate.

Television, McLuhan called "cool." Everything we receive from TV is as if it were part of our most comfortable surroundings. We greet TV coverage as if it is part of us and we lose track of where we end and where the news event starts. McLuhan's slant on TV news says we find TV so palatable that we swallow it without realizing it is now inside us. In other words, all that threatening information is now part of our internal view of the outside world, and today that world is as scary as anything is. This dramatic crime and violence brought into our homes by media can lead us to believe we must strike out against others—and those of a different rank are safe targets.

*Scared into buying.* Those who wish to control markets use fear to sell their wares. Some sales pitches depend on raising fears. Your life will be shortened if you do not purchase this diet. Vote for the opposing candidate and life-as-you-know-it will crumble. Pratkanis and Aronson, who wrote about fear as a propaganda technique, offered further examples from life insurance and drug sales.[14] Just look at magazine, newspaper, or television advertisements to see how fear is used.

Advertisers and propagandists also appeal to rankism to sell their products. If you wear these clothes, you will be Somebody. Do not use our deodorant and you are a Nobody. Vote for our candidate and the Nobodies will be removed from the public trough.

Unlike entertainment, which merely titillates us, sales pitches and propaganda can prey on our most basic fears. With all these attempts to frighten us, we need to confront our fears.

### Facing Our Fears

As a child, I walked with my school class to town hall for vaccinations. They lined us up alphabetically by last name and I was always second in line for my class. (That was before I took my husband's Wambach name.) Only the fellow up front avoided the trauma of my ordeal. The first time I saw the needle, I fainted. On later trips, I trembled during the three-block walk. By the time I faced the needle, I was so nauseous I threw up, then I fainted. This was not a good way to make friends. I remember being put at the end of the line, thus sparing my classmates who had been conducting themselves with calm resignation. The irony is I have been diabetic for over half my life. I have learned to take several shots daily and never flinch. I had no choice but to face my fear of needles.

Dread of facing our fears adds to our angst. "People will do anything, no matter how absurd, in order to avoid facing their own soul,"[15] wrote Carl G. Jung. It is hard work to pretend our battles between Somebodies and Nobodies causes us no trepidation. The energy we devote to avoiding scary stuff is energy we could more productively be focusing on stopping rankism.

Those who tell you they are never afraid have yet to identify their fears. Yes, it is possible to experience fear and not notice the emotion on a conscious level, but it would be better for us to take a little time, look inward, and understand our personal fears. Refusing to look at our own fears is akin to seeing ourselves as victim. We dig in our heels and spurn all overtures to grow.

## Chapter Summary

In this chapter, we have looked at fear as a basic component of rankism. Fear is, first, a gift that signals us that danger is near. While some fears are real, not all are. Unrealistic fears consist of specific phobias and general anxiety. We not only shun fear, but we are drawn to it as entertainment. Our society is besieged with induced fear beyond that which is entertaining. Media news, sales promotions, and propaganda all tap our natural fears and fan them for reasons beyond our own good. A special fear is that which keeps us from facing what personally scares us most. It is not possible to understand rankism unless we look inside at our own will to power and our own fears. Only then can we move toward right-rank.

We can learn to identify our fears and curtail our unreasonable push for power over others. Rollo May, a psychologist, found that violence comes from a person's "repressed anger, rage, combined with constant fear"[16] of powerlessness. These are people who are told they are worthless, and there is nothing they can do about it. Bertrand Russell warned us: "Collective fear stimulates herd instinct and tends to produce ferocity toward those who are not regarded as members of the herd." We have so much to gain by confronting fear.

**Reaching for Right-Rank: When I am Afraid, I _____**

Spend some quiet time on each of the following. How would you complete these sentences that begin with, When I am afraid...

My body changes include _____

I feel _____

My thoughts turn to _____

I want to _____

My behavior becomes _____

I do _____

I get frightened when _____

I try to handle my fear by _____

# Part Three

# A Lineup of Rankists

In a battle between Somebodies and Nobodies, any of us might present ourselves as one or more of the types presented here. I concentrate in Chapters Six and Seven on blatantly abusive traits. For each trait, you will find a description of the type and ways to identify them. In Chapter Eight, we will look more deeply into what constitutes each of these types, since they all have both strengths and weaknesses.

*Rankist types.* The type system I use in Chapters Six and Seven is another tool for helping you understand and stop rankism in your life. Types are complex explanations of how one's actions can be identified as rankist.

*Overt and covert.* I have separated rankist types into overt classes, where actions can be observed easily, and covert classes, where actions are hidden or more subtle.

*Somebody Rankists.* Somebody Rankists hold onto their positions of power by preventing others from progressing.

*Nobody Rankists.* Nobody Rankists respond to oppression with acts designed to harm Somebody Rankists and/or the system they share.

*Right-rank types.* Nestled among the overt Nobody Rankists you will find two types that practice right-rank. These are clear, straightforward examples of right-rank.

Try not to get bogged down by all this negative stuff. After these three chapters, you will learn how all this will help you reach your own brand of right-rank.

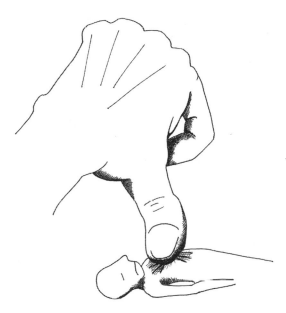

## CHAPTER SIX

# *Somebody Rankists: Those Who Obstruct*

"**I**'ve seen the enemy and it is us," proclaimed the cartoon opossum Pogo. In the 1950s, Walt Kelly created Pogo, who lived in the Okefenokee Swamp, to comment on the way we function in our world. Pogo characters were always trying to find the enemy, and they did not realize they were their own favorite foe. Somebody Rankists protect their place at the top by obstructing anyone of lesser power. In the end, these impediments do not necessarily help Somebodies. The variety of Somebody Rankist conflict strategies will be familiar.

Karl, who worked for the same company for twenty-eight years, encountered Somebody Rankists in his company. In the beginning, he was given night hours—except on holidays, when he worked both days and nights. That was no real problem for Karl, who knew he had to prove himself to his new employers.

As years progressed, Karl married, had children, and was involved in their school and athletic events. He was promoted and had a say about his work hours. Whereas once he had no vacations, later he had holidays and two full weeks off work in summer. His family spent that time together with shared hometown activities and an occasional trip.

Karl considered himself fortunate. The work was not always challenging or exciting, but he did what he thought was his duty, and his family was healthy and happy.

Then, things changed in ways Karl could not understand. The business was sold and the new owners seemed unaware of the contributions that Karl and his colleagues made. Karl was told he must vacation at times convenient for the company, times when his wife could not join him. He received work assignments on weekends, then nights.

Worst of all, Karl was given work he had long outgrown, work suited to newcomers with little experience. Furthermore, the new bosses criticized his performance on these entry-level jobs. Karl was both angry and humiliated to find himself no longer valued. The stress was making him ill and every day he dreaded going to the work. One Friday morning in November, Karl was notified that this was his last day and that, of course, he would receive a nice severance package. Bewildered, Karl asked, "What the hell happened?"

We do not have enough information from Karl's account to know the full story of his job loss. He is not alone as others ask the same, "What the hell happened?" question about events in their family, personal relationships, work, or community group. Sometimes, we all have trouble grasping exactly what took place.

In order to understand Somebody Rankists, I present several examples of how those in power move to protect their positions. These types of Somebody Rankists are not mutually exclusive. One type may share characteristics with another type. If you are applying these types to someone you know—even to yourself—you may find that some individuals share more than one rankist type.

Rankist designations will be based on the abusers' expression of behavior, either overt (open) or covert (more hidden). Each rankist type can be identified by behaviors, emotions, a typical line that sums up this type, expectations the type has of others, and how targets respond to this rankist type.

## Overt Somebody Rankists

Overt rank abusers are somewhat easier to recognize than others because they operate out front and we can identify them from their expressions, if only we know what to heed. Overt Somebody Rankists maintain control of their position by communicating in one direction—from the top down. Overt Somebody Rankists do not trust any sort of feedback from those they consider beneath them.

*Tyrant.* Elizabeth Becker, then of the *Washington Post*, met Pol Pot at his headquarters in 1978 when he was prime minister of Cambodia. In the course of his regime, 1975–1979, Pol Pot's Khmer Rouge army killed over a million of their fellow citizens. Becker said Pol Pot sat quietly before the audience of which she was the only Western journalist. His gestures were almost dainty. For over an hour, he ranted and raved, "always in the quietest tones."

The night of her visit, Pol Pot's guards came to the guesthouse where she and other visitors slept. The guards threatened them all and killed her colleague, the British academic

Malcolm Caldwell. Becker said she could not convey how Pol Pot's contradictory behavior engendered such a depth of fear among her group.[1] And yet, because of his gentility, other governments were not convinced Pol Pot was dangerous.

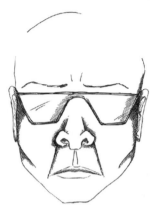

---

### TYRANT

| | |
|---|---|
| Behaviors: | Still, intense eye contact, quiet voice, measured words |
| Emotions: | Flat, enjoys being in control, pretends to be calm, secretly fears others |
| Typical line: | "Of course, you will do things my way, won't you." |
| Expects others to: | Obey, conform |
| Response of targets: | Terrified, compliant, imprisoned |

---

Using force in a steely, premeditated fashion, the Tyrant stands quietly without blinking and talks in calm, modulated tones without facial expression. Intimidation comes from our clear understanding that the Tyrant will not hesitate to use physical or emotional force. Not because the Tyrant is angry, but because the Tyrant will carefully devise and execute whatever plan is necessary to gain compliance from others.

The Tyrant is oppressive in demanding specified robotic behavior from others. If someone is noncompliant or inexact, the Tyrant exacts severe retribution.

In old-fashioned schools, teachers expected students to sit quietly, answer questions correctly, and concentrate only on the teacher's presentation of the immediate lesson. Tyrant schoolmasters thought it their duty to tolerate no nonsense from children. Tyrants can also be found at home in the form of militaristic parents who expect children to be seen and not heard.

The British actor Michael Caine offered a striking portrayal of a Tyrant in the 1997 movie *Shadow Run*, which is now available on DVD. Caine's unflinching stare makes audiences want to squirm, but they sit there riveted with fear.

Tyrants are fearful of others, and they lack sufficient skills to lead. Taking no chance of exposing their weaknesses, Tyrants treat life as if everyone is a pawn on their chessboard.

*Seething Giant.* For a few years, I worked to organize a political group of volunteers devoted to concerns of the elderly, especially those who could not advocate for themselves. Shortly after a new person assumed leadership of the group, I attended a meeting of ten people responsible for the group's direction. Immediately, the new leader launched into a diatribe about what was wrong with our performance. When I asked the new leader to clarify an issue, he turned his fury on me. He said that my direction of one committee was ill conceived, that I had never contributed anything worthwhile, and on and on.

I was dumbfounded. As I attempted to contain my confusion, I tried to understand what might have precipitated this level of displeasure. Most of all, I was surprised that everyone at the meeting, both paid and volunteer workers, sat mute throughout his tirade. Before I left that meeting, I knew this was my last affiliation with the group, for I felt betrayed by everyone present. The following day, I submitted my resignation.

A few years later, I heard from a volunteer who did not attend that meeting, that such harangues by the leader—often directed at one person—happened with some frequency. Each time, not one of those present registered a complaint that he treated people so shabbily. Not until I began to work on this book did I finally understand what sort of rankist that leader was.

### SEETHING GIANT

| | |
|---|---|
| Behaviors: | Screams, face flushes, arms flail |
| Emotions: | Excitable, angry, out of control, hostile |
| Typical line: | "What the x/#** are you doing, you %/*#!" |
| Expects others to: | Tremble, obey |
| Response of targets: | Alarmed, confused, immobile, intimidated |

The Seething Giant uses anger to keep others on guard as they attempt to predict when the malicious fury will erupt. High-intensity outbursts and insulting language may or may not be precipitated by something in the immediate moment. If the anger is associated with others' behavior, the Seething

Giant overreacts. We have all been annoyed by someone else's driving, yet automobile operators who engage in road rage put everyone at risk.

The Seething Giant is sometimes part of the cycle of domestic violence. Family members never know what brings on the storm, and they tend to think they are responsible. The Seething Giant can also disrupt the workplace. My guess is that the leader who spewed his venom at me enacted that same scene many times during his career. As my experience showed, recipients of such anger or those who observe others receiving the ferocity of the Seething Giant are often paralyzed. So, the behavior of the Seething Giant continues unchallenged.

The Seething Giant may lack impulse control, and be easily moved to anger, or, the anger may be merely a tool for emotionally abusing others. Seething Giants fear they will not be able to handle the situation, and so they aggressively take charge through intimidation.

*Gangster.* Cheryl had been a friend of Jim's throughout the eight years she had worked for her present company. She considered him good at his job, enthusiastic about meeting his monthly goals, and fun at company get-togethers. It was strange for her when she began to hear others call Jim a problem. Cheryl was not sure of the specifics, but she decided it would be best not to invite him to her wedding.

When she returned to work from her honeymoon, Cheryl noticed that Jim skipped the company holiday party and was starting to miss work regularly. Rumors were that he was sick all the time and not meeting his goals.

Then the company let Jim go. No one heard much more about it other than that he had received poor evaluations and his boss wanted him gone.

Later on Cheryl ran into Jim at a restaurant. He was bitter about what had happened. Jim told her that everyone had ganged up on him. Those he counted as friends had started avoiding him. He had started having panic attacks and was sick all the time.

Well, Cheryl told me, Jim's departure was good for the company. When I suggested to Cheryl that she had participated as a gangster, she became agitated with me. I have observed close-hand other instances of Gangster action. Every time, those involved refused to consider that they may have encouraged others to be part of the sinister ousting of a group member.

---

### GANGSTER

| | |
|---|---|
| Behaviors: | As the group turns against the Nobody, sneers, rolls eyes, scoffs |
| Emotions: | Within the group—some feel powerful, some are ambivalent, some are anxious |
| Typical line: | "If we get rid of that one, we'll all be fine." |
| Expects others to: | Join the gang or get pushed out |
| Response of targets: | Bewildered, lonely, betrayed, beaten |

---

The Gangster uses others to enforce his or her hold on rank. If someone in the group disagrees with or threatens the

Gangster, it is the other members who push the disputant back into place or out the door. Whistleblowers find Gangsters are often shoving them into submission.

Heinz Leymann used the term "mobbing" to describe what happened to Jim. Even those, like Cheryl, who become gangsters do not recognize their role in pushing someone from the group. Mobbing entails emotional abuse inflicted by a group. In some parts of Europe, personnel departments are trained to identify and stop mobbing. While sexual harassment and discrimination of protected groups are illegal in the United States, mobbing is neither labeled nor forbidden.[2]

Gangsters can be found in families, too. David Pelzer's book, *A Child Called "It,"* about his abused childhood is difficult to read, but anyone who picks it up reads every descriptive page. David's alcoholic mother had other children and chose only David to be isolated from his siblings. She played sick and torturous games with him, and the other children even laughed at his pain. David's gangster mother wanted him out of the family, and finally a school nurse helped him to leave that home.[3]

Gangsters do not trust that they can work successfully with others. Lacking the skills to change the relationship and any respect for the person's worth, Gangsters elect to maneuver others into tossing the Nobody out—and not until the individual is put down, demoralized, and badly beaten.

*Sovereign.* Joseph Stalin, Russian dictator from 1929–1953, designed elaborate mechanisms to ensure that no one disagreed with him. That included not only the individuals close to him, but also every person in Russia. In 1937, the section of his government called the NKVD (People's Commissariat of Internal Affairs) devised an elaborate system of informers throughout the country. Those who were paid and promoted for fingering suspicious citizens were powerful in their communities. Citizens competed to be informers. A distinguished section of the NKVD enforced loyalty. And there was a "supersecret special section to keep an eye on the secret special section."[4]

---

**SOVEREIGN**

| | |
|---|---|
| Behaviors: | Turns people against one another, enforces rigid rules |
| Emotions: | Suspicious, paranoid, sadistic |
| Typical line: | "You are either for us or against us." |
| Expects others to: | Show no dissent, no self-expression, total loyalty |
| Response of targets: | Cautious, tentative, avoid sensitive topics |

---

The Sovereign expects to be in total control and manages command by surrounding him or herself with those who never question the Sovereign's authority. Hiring and promoting the most competent person does not happen. Rather, those who flourish do so because of their unquestioning loyalty to the rank abuser. It is amidst the Sovereign's rule that we find nepotism, cronyism, favoritism, and ever so many "kiss-ups."

The Sovereign is sometimes head of a family business. Brothers and cousins can be trusted to protect family members.

Those who are not blood relatives can survive only if they prove they will always stand with the owner against any outside interference. That is difficult to accomplish, and may strain an individual's sense of right doing.

The Sovereign sometimes couches the demand for unquestioning adherence in the favorable term, loyalty. What distinguishes the Sovereign's strategy, however, is that disagreement is not allowed. To disagree—to question—is to reveal oneself as an outsider.

The concept of groupthink explains how a Sovereign can undermine not only individuals, but also the organization of which all are part.[5] Decisions are made without looking at all information, without considering many alternatives, without consulting experts. Rather, the Sovereign convinces loyalists they are unified and unbeatable, and their cause is commendable. When the plan fails, the Sovereign's group rationalizes their poor decisions. Imagine the political decisions made when a leader is a Sovereign and uses groupthink.

*Grandee.* L. Dennis Kozlowski was indicted for embezzling six hundred million dollars from Tyco. Facts about his purchases with unauthorized company loans were mind-boggling. He reportedly used Tyco money to pay six million dollars for redecoration and another six million on paintings for his Manhattan apartment. He spent another five million dollars for a ring.[6]

At his first trial, jurors were shown videos of another eighteen-million-dollar apartment that included—among other extravagances—a fifteen-thousand-dollar umbrella stand and a seventeen-thousand-dollar toilette box. All of which was paid for by company funds. Jurors also viewed scenes from a two-million-dollar birthday party for Kozlowski's wife. Company funds paid for half of that.[7] In June 2005, Kozlowski and Tyco's former finance chief Mark H. Swartz were found guilty of grand larceny, falsifying business records, and securities fraud for plundering over six hundred million dollars from the company.

Somewhere during his career, Kozlowski decided that Tyco was his personal domain, not a business entity created and maintained by the combined effort and funds of thousands of individuals.

| | **GRANDEE** |
|---|---|
| Behaviors: | Stuck-up, ignores others, flaunts possessions and positions |
| Emotions: | Self-centered, eager to impress others |
| Typical line: | "I am the center of the world, and the rest of you are here to praise and serve me." |
| Expects others to: | Stay hidden, be in awe, envy |
| Response of targets: | Spurned, irritated, weary |

Grandees consider themselves the center of the universe. Psychologists call Grandees narcissistic. They are interested only in themselves and assume everyone else is devoted entirely to them. The Grandee arrogantly promotes self. More than that, Grandees do this at the expense of others because they do not consider anyone else's rights or feelings. Never expect a Grandee to show concern for others, because everyone exists only to serve the Grandee.

Instead of accepting obligations, Grandees flaunt perquisites that come with their rank. Instead of driving a Chevrolet company car, the Grandee covets a Porsche. While the family struggles to put food on the table, the Grandee adorns expensive designer clothes. The Grandee openly disobeys rules, and laughs when others stand in line, wait for the traffic light to change, or insist on an honest audit. Grandees assume they exist for only the top spot.

Grandees are not only selfish. They also fear that they cannot excel by working with others, so they separate themselves from the very environment that could offer them success. Instead, Grandees create an alternate world that is not part of their immediate surroundings.

### Covert Somebody Rankists

Covert rank abusers are more difficult to identify because their expression is subtler, more hidden. If you know how to recognize their disguises, however, real covert rank abusers are easy to identify.

*Extortionist.* When reports of female cadets became known, an investigation found alarming examples of rankism in military schools. According to a 1994 General Accounting Office report, fifty to seventy-five percent of women cadets at the Air Force Academy, Naval Academy, and West Point said they experienced sexual harassment once or twice a month at their military institutions. The report defined sexual harassment as "words, gestures, or actions with sexual connotations which are unwelcome and tend to intimidate, alarm, or abuse another person."[8]

The Department of Defense later surveyed 579 Air Force female cadets. Of those questioned, 109 (nineteen percent) reported being targets of sexual assault. This is not harassment, but actual sexual assault, defined as "the touching of another without their consent in a sexual manner, including attempts, in order to arouse, appeal to, or gratify the lust or sexual desire of the accused, the victim, or both." Forty-three of the female cadets (seven percent) were targets of rape or attempted rape.[9]

Most women opted not to report the incidents because they feared reprisals by upper classmen or commanders.

---

### EXTORTIONIST

| | |
|---|---|
| Behaviors: | Invades others' space, pretends to mentor, enhances self at the Nobody's expense |
| Emotions: | Feels entitled, enjoys others' distress |
| Typical line: | "You owe it to me." |
| Expects others to: | Be grateful and surrender their self-respect |
| Response of targets: | Manipulated, degraded, cheated |

---

We expect a mentor to guide and teach those who are less experienced and less knowledgeable. Instead, the Extortionist uses the special relationship, designed to pass on skills and wisdom, to manipulate the mentored person like a puppet.

The Extortionist helps apprentices, but at a price beyond genuine gratefulness. An Extortionist's unreasonable demand is very clear to the person being propositioned. The only subtlety is that the Extortionist exacts payment for favors away from public view. Demands for sexual favors, embezzlement, or theft are unreasonable, and such requirements diminish the subordinate, the Nobody.

Rather than assist the new person, Extortionists use the situation for their own profit at the expense of the other.

*Scapegoater.* In 1940, as European Jews were being sent to the Warsaw ghetto, so the United States was compiling the names of Japanese in our country. In 1941, as Jews were being rounded up in Paris and sent to labor camps, so those of Japanese ancestry were put under Federal control soon after Japan bombed Pearl Harbor and America entered the war. By 1942, sixty-three percent of the individuals of Japanese heritage on the government's list were American citizens. All were taken to internment camps in Idaho, Montana, Nevada, Utah, Oregon, Colorado, New Mexico, Wyoming, Washington, Arizona, California, North Dakota, Arkansas and Texas. When they left their homes, prisoners took with them only what they could carry. In the camps, they were required to live in crowded conditions and work in beet and potato fields.

In 1943, as Jews in the Warsaw ghetto revolted, inmates in Japanese American internment camps began labor strikes. Reversing itself in 1944, the U. S. Government decided that

Japanese Americans were now eligible for the draft. Those who resisted and refused to serve were indicted.

Most of the one hundred and twenty thousand interned Japanese Americans lost everything they had owned. When they finally were allowed to return home, their property and goods were gone. In 1988, the Federal Government awarded $20,000 and a Presidential apology to each interned Japanese American.[10]

On December 10, 1999, Wen Ho Lee, a scientist at Los Alamos National Laboratory was charged with fifty-nine counts of spying for China. Lee, a Chinese American, born in Taiwan, was imprisoned for nine months—much of that time in solitary confinement—on what turned out to be a very thin case. Among the groups of scientists, Asian-American activists, and religious groups that voiced public support for Lee, a newly created national network was born—the Coalition Against Racial and Ethnic Scapegoating, CARES. Lee eventually pleaded guilty to one of the counts and the judge issued a public apology.[11]

The 660 inmates held by the U.S. Government at the U. S. Naval Base on Guantanamo Bay did not have access to attorneys and advocacy groups as did Wen Ho Lee. The prison, set up in January 2002, held non-Americans from forty-two countries who allegedly worked against the United States in Afghanistan. Because the Government declared they were not prisoners-of-war, but "enemy combatants," none were protected by the Geneva Convention that stipulates the terms and conditions under which prisoners may be held or treated. Among other things that meant they had no right to counsel or trial, no right to communicate with family, and that they could be held indefinitely. Even their names were not available.[12]

---

### SCAPEGOATER

| | |
|---|---|
| Behaviors: | Diverts attention, not accountable, preys on vulnerable Nobodies |
| Emotions: | Feels crafty, hates criticism of self, prejudiced |
| Typical line: | "Someone else is to blame." |
| Expects others to: | Be distracted from responsible Somebodies |
| Response of targets: | Victimized, defensive, deceived |

---

A Scapegoater is one who transfers blame to persons or groups, who are not necessarily guilty, in order to focus attention away from those who are actually responsible—sometimes from themselves—or because the true culprits cannot be apprehended. Scapegoats can be conveniently created distractions from other activities that the Scapegoater wants to go unnoticed. Just as rank brings the power to credit individuals and groups for success, so rank also allows one to affix blame. Scapegoaters abuse this power by using others as patsies for their own shortcomings, thus keeping one's own rank at the expense of others.

Scapegoaters are everywhere. They are the athletes who blame a coach or referee, the students who attribute their failures to teachers or schools, the criminals who blame their parents. Accepting responsibility for one's own shortcomings is difficult for most of us. When we select others to answer for our mistakes, it is an aggressive form of rank abuse.

*Fabricator.* That Lawrence Berkeley National Laboratory found that one of its scientists had falsified data was big news in the medical community. The Office of Research Integrity of the U. S. Department of Health and Human Services verified the results of the laboratory's investigation. Robert P. Liburdy was found guilty of "scientific misconduct in biomedical research by intentionally falsifying and fabricating data and claims" in two scientific papers reporting his biomedical research.[13]

---

**FABRICATOR**

| | |
|---|---|
| Behaviors: | Pretends to be a different Somebody, lies, plagiarizes, steals, gets ahead on someone else's work |
| Emotions: | Feels smarter than others, enjoys own deviousness, fears own incompetence |
| Typical line: | "This is my work. Really." |
| Expects others to: | Be fooled, give the Fabricator credit for another's work |
| Response of targets: | Let down, robbed, misled |

---

The Fabricator is one who poses as something he or she is not. Pretending to create and/or distribute services, items, or information, the Fabricator passes on misrepresentations of real things. By manufacturing data to suit his own conclusions, Dr. Liburdy violated the trust we give researchers who are supposed to advance learning.

Fabricators can also abuse rank by presenting others' work as their own, thus keeping subordinates from advancement they deserve. This is the "show horse" that accepts accolades for others' accomplishments and never credits the "work horses" whose labor generated the success.

The Fabricator, same as the Extortionist, may also be a mentor. The difference between the two is that Extortionists pretend to teach and support the ones they are mentoring, even while they are mistreating them. Because Fabricators realize their rank depends on the gifts of the ones they are mentoring, they steal the apprentice's work or refuse to credit them.

This tactic can go unnoticed for some time because those tied to the Fabricator may consider it usual that one with a superior position deserves all the credit. If the Fabricator is exposed, results can be dangerous for everyone.

*Gatekeeper.* Consider the equipment for which a theater tech is responsible—lights, cables, microphones, audio and video recorders, projectors, screens, curtains, ladders, flats, saws, drills, hammers, paints, brushes, makeup, costumes. The full equipment list for any theater would fill many pages.

What happens when those who share a theater space realize that the list provided by the head technician is woefully incomplete? They hear the technician repeat, "I keep the inventory in my head. Just ask if you need something."

What happens? Thespians stay on the technical person's good side and continue to ask for whatever they need, even when it makes everyone else's job increasingly more difficult.

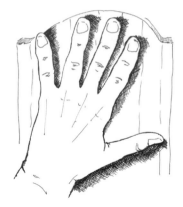

---

**GATEKEEPER**

| | |
|---|---|
| Behaviors: | Erects barriers between people and things, controls entry, withholds information, chooses favorites |
| Emotions: | Feels more confident surrounded by objects, happiest when controlling others, proud of selectiveness |
| Typical line: | "I permit access only if I choose." |
| Expects others to: | Kowtow to gain entree to that which is rightfully theirs, ask permission |
| Response of targets: | Resentful, try to please |

---

Because of their position, some rankists are able to control others' access to persons, items, information, or opportunities necessary to maintain and increase their own rank. The Gatekeeper is a powerful, though seldom a high-profile person within a group. Gatekeepers abuse their role when they dispense and withhold necessary items and information in order to maintain their own rank, keep others indebted, and chasten those they wish to punish.

Those who provide access are everywhere. Parents control who calls and visits their home. Administrative Assistants control who sees the boss. Schedulers decide who sees the doctor or other professional. Every one of these positions is necessary. Those who guard the entrances may make the best decisions they can. The rankist Gatekeeper makes decisions designed to keep others down, and sometimes to keep their own superiors from being well or fully informed. They offer passage based on selfish reasons as opposed to what is best for individuals and the whole. Their decisions are designed to hang onto their Gatekeeper power.

*Snubber.* Hattie, my mother-in-law, was over ninety years old when she moved to a nice apartment in an assisted living facility. Her health was quite good and she was very alert. When she first moved to the apartment, I was struck by one staff member, who stopped by while the family was visiting. Rather than acknowledge Hattie, who was sitting at her table, the staff person walked past her. Leaning toward us to shake our hands, the employee then sat down, took out her pad and pen, and said, "Let's decide what she needs."

During the interview, we frequently looked at Hattie and said things such as, "Which meal seating time would you like?" and "Do you want someone to regularly change your sheets?"

Even when Hattie answered us, the staff member never looked at her. After she left, I asked Hattie how she felt about her decisions. "I kept looking at my hands to be sure I was here," she commented.

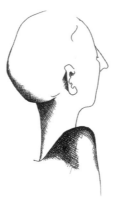

---

### SNUBBER

| | |
|---|---|
| Behaviors: | Looks through a Nobody, talks to others about Nobodies as if they aren't even there |
| Emotions: | Feels separate, disconnected from others, unaware of being patronizing |
| Typical line: | "We can talk about those Nobodies even in their presence because they don't count." |
| Expects others to: | Be grateful, forget the ignored person |
| Response of Targets: | Invisible, befuddled, cut off. |

---

The Snubber treats those they consider of lower rank with indifference. Underlings do not exist. To any of us, to be overlooked is as disconcerting, maybe more so, than overt hostility. Our need for recognition is basic to understanding who we are.

We hear stories of servants who are talked about as if they were not present. Others are treated as though they are invisible. Children, the elderly, the mentally ill, those who live on the streets are examples of humans who are snubbed regularly.

An important thing to remember about Snubbers is that their strategy helps them stay aloof. At first glance, it may seem the slighted person ceases to exist. In actuality, it is the Snubber who has withdrawn. Sensing some threat, Snubbers stay separate from their surroundings and those they consider Nobodies.

**Chapter Summary**

For every Somebody Rankist, there was a box with the most obvious identifications. *Overt* Somebody Rankists include those in power whose abusive tactics are broad and apparent. They include:

- Tyrants, who without emotion do everything necessary to make underlings obey;
- Seething Giants, who use angry outbursts to intimidate others into submission;
- Gangsters, who use others—often without their knowledge—to keep dissenters in line or push them out the door;
- Sovereigns, who design a system that ensures loyalty at the expense of the greater good; and
- Grandees, who take advantage of their position so that others support their lavish lifestyle.

*Covert* Somebody Rankists are abusers of position whose actions are less readily apparent. They are:

- Extortionists, who extract wrongful actions in exchange for mentorship;
- Scapegoaters, who blame others to distract attention from their own mistakes, or because the true culprits are not readily apprehensible;
- Fabricators, feigning a legitimate position, who nefariously lie and steal;

- Gatekeepers, who award access to individuals and services solely to meet their own personal needs; and
- Snubbers, who ignore those they consider to be lesser than they are.

Together, these are types of individuals who misuse their higher positions of power. In so doing, they treat others as Nobodies. The next chapter includes rankists, all down the power line, who have been dealt with as Nobodies, and then misuse their position.

**Reaching for Right-Rank: Somebody Rankists You Know**

1.  According to this chapter, why might a Somebody Rankist fit into more than one rankist type? (Here is a hint. All are based on the way those in power respond to threat. Is it possible to have more than one reaction?)
2.  What is the difference between overt rankist types and covert rankist types?
3.  Think of examples from your life of any of the rankist types discussed in this chapter.
4.  Do you recall ever using any of these rankist maneuvers yourself?

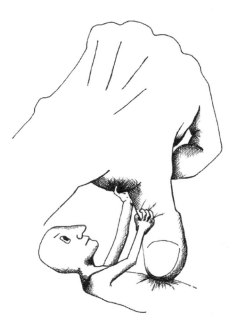

## CHAPTER SEVEN

# *Nobody Rankists:*
# *Those Who Counter*

Some Nobody Rankists are born to a lowly position. Their parents are poor; their schools are under funded; their neighborhoods are peopled with those who have given up after a lifetime of failure. Around these unfortunates of society are the makings of rebellion and violence. Yet, anyone can feel like a Nobody.

*Karl weighs his options.* Karl lived a comfortable middle class American life and never thought about being a Nobody. Then, his life changed. The last months at work were terrible for Karl. He was relegated to jobs that required no training and way less than his experience. As he struggled to understand what was happening, he was discharged. After twenty-eight years with the company, he was told his services were no longer needed. What was he to do?

Karl admitted to me that his first thoughts were to plant an explosive in the building. He knew where to put it and could certainly figure out how to create such a device. He would not seriously pursue such a thing, but it was his first thought. Had he belonged to a union, Karl would have headed for their office. At age fifty-six, he had no idea how to look for a new job.

It was Karl's neighbor who suggested he see a lawyer, that there were laws against firing people, especially older employees. Karl thought that was a good way for him to start.

Karl's immediate inclination to act with violence is not unusual. "Deeds of violence in our society are performed largely by those trying to establish their self-esteem, to defend their self-image, and to demonstrate that they, too, are significant," wrote Rollo May.[1] Violence is the extreme form of rankism.

To a Nobody, subordinate types of rankism may seem to offer an immediate sense of justice. Just like other forms of rankism, violence can transform a person. Again, remember that the Nobody Rankist and right-rank types I present here are not mutually exclusive and not necessarily complete. That means you may recognize yourself or others in several types.

## Overt Nobody Rankists

Anyone can recognize overt reactions from targets of rank abuse. Overt Nobody Rankists may not weigh the wisdom of assaulting another.

*Retaliator.* Some say it started when Floyd Hatfield pilfered a Randall McCoy pig. Some say it was more than bad blood, that the McCoys were jealous of the Hatfields' economic prosperity.[2] Others insist there was an unwed pregnancy between youngsters of the rival families. Whatever the reasons, when a McCoy was gunned down, you could be sure one of the Hatfield gang would soon be shot. Everyone agrees that the thirty-year feud between the Hatfields of West Virginia and the McCoys of Kentucky ended numerous lives on both sides.

---

### RETALIATOR

| | |
|---|---|
| Behaviors: | Counters abuse with identical mistreatment, plans carefully |
| Emotions: | Harbors rancor, believes in an eye for an eye |
| Typical line: | "Those Somebodies will get their due." |
| Expects others to: | Watch their backs, get what they deserve |
| Response of targets: | Uncertainty, vigilance, more retribution |

---

The Retaliator strikes back in kind. If the Seething Giant fumes and stomps about the room, the Retaliator screams, "You may think you've won, but you haven't heard the last of this." The game for the Retaliator is tit for tat.

If the Gatekeeper blocks access to necessary information, the Retaliator will find a way to keep information from the Gatekeeper rankist. The Retaliator is capable of acting like any of the rank abusers, only in reverse. This is the person who says, "Don't get mad. Get even."

It is as though Retaliators sense the balance of justice has just made their side lighter. Their immediate task is to remove an in-kind weight from the side that offended them. The Retaliator is a fighter who will be strongest, no matter the cost.

In extreme cases, Retaliators will even hurt those outside their immediate target to achieve their goal. Consider contemporary wars between Israel and Palestine. For both, violence continues as repayment against the other country's destructive response to a previous act of violence by the other. It is like Hatfield and McCoy on a bigger scale.

The same cycle of violence can be found among street gangs, between union and management, among domestic partners—even among neighbors in a cul de sac. Retaliators are afraid that if they are not in control, not right, not tough, someone will take advantage.

*Dog-Kicker.* Unhappy and insecure in her job, Jean fell into a pattern of yelling at her husband and children every time the family was together. Her husband, Andy, had told her that if she refused to go to counseling, he and the kids were leaving. Only after the school's principle informed Andy and her that their nine-year-old son had skipped school and been picked up for stealing a pair of shirts from a local merchant did Jean realize she had been too unhappy to notice the mounting family problems.

---

### DOG-KICKER

| | |
|---|---|
| Behaviors: | Hurt by a Somebody, so wounds the defenseless |
| Emotions: | Confused about source of injury, fearful, regretful |
| Typical line: | "You make me so angry, you stupid dope." |
| Expects others to: | Help Dog-Kicker feel better |
| Response of targets: | Frightened, puzzled, cowering |

---

Rather than strike back directly at the rank abuser, the Dog-Kicker chooses someone more vulnerable and mistreats that person. The Dog-Kicker ends up with fear from two sources: first, from the original situation, and second, from the displaced area. Jean had been terrified about what was happening at work. She lacked the skills to deal with the mounting pressure. Her unreflective response had been to attack those she figured would not turn on her. When Andy challenged her actions and when her son began to act out, Jean was squeezed from many directions.

The Dog-Kicker is a Seething Giant who displaces anger onto others. Feeling like a Nobody in one situation, the

Dog-Kicker becomes a Somebody Rankist in a different place. The person who has been kicked has no idea why, and may not realize the anger comes from somewhere else. What can happen as a result is that the newly abused Nobody will turn around and start abusing someone else—and the cycle of rankism spreads.

*Flatterer.* The Nixon tapes are records of the interactions between the President and those who worked for him. As Richard Nixon talked loudly, sometimes we cannot tell if his staff or Cabinet members were talking back or simply assumed to be nodding. There are moments of silence as Nixon is clearly speaking to John Haldeman, John Erlichmann, or Henry Kissinger. Other times, we hear from his aides as they restate and agree with everything their President says.[3]

### FLATTERER

| | |
|---|---|
| Behaviors: | Obedient, makes self irreplaceable, pretends to respect a Somebody, demeans self |
| Emotions: | Anxious to please, dependent, unsure |
| Typical line: | "I would be nothing without my favorite Somebody, who protects me!" |
| Expects others to: | Be impressed by flatterer, to gain closeness to a Somebody, to be envied |
| Response of targets: | Disgust, sympathy, irritation |

Rather than strike back, Flatterers compliment the rank abuser, hoping to gain protection from the powerful Somebody Rankist their flattery enhances. Flatterers know they are weak and dependent. They survive conflict by being generous and humble toward those who will safeguard them.

The adulation is probably less than genuine. Flatterers are sometimes described as "suck-ups," or "yes-men," or "brown-nosers." They may not like those who wield power, but they would rather emphasize the positive. If you want to know the good qualities of a Somebody Rankist (and there is always something positive about everyone), ask a Flatterer.

Most of all, Flatterers want to be accepted, to be part of the group. To ensure their own place, they are quite willing to subordinate themselves to those more powerful.

## Right-Rank Types

Right-rank types are the Overt Nobodies who can teach us how to effectively deal with Somebody rank abusers. There are numerous ways to demonstrate your right-rank. Every time you recognize someone of a different rank as a person who deserves dignity, you are of right-rank. If you stand up for yourself when a rankist treats you badly, you are of right-rank. So you may recognize these traits in yourself and others, I offer two more developed types of right-rank.

*Persuader.* During the 1980s, Swedish researcher Heinz Leymann studied mobbing in the workplace. "Mobbing" is the term he gave to a systematic effort by one or more individuals to drive someone from a workplace. You may remember his work from discussion of the Gangster type in the previous chapter.

More than just understanding the way people were pushed out of their jobs, Leymann found himself convincing companies that mobbing was harmful to individuals and to business. Because of Dr. Leymann's work, more companies now have training programs to help identify and eliminate mobbing. In Australia and Sweden, as well as in some European cities, mobbing is illegal. Someday, mobbing against those who are not sufficiently protected by laws against age and race discrimination may be also be enacted in the United States.[4]

### PERSUADER

| | |
|---|---|
| Behaviors: | Organized, prepared, communication and interpersonal skills, public speaker |
| Emotions: | Courageous, caring, respectful |
| Typical line: | "If we all work together, everyone can win." |
| Expects others to: | Be reluctant at first, hopeful, try a better way |
| Response of targets: | Unsure, need to be convinced |

The Persuader is one example of right-rank. Persuaders appeal to rankist or others connected with conflict situations that abuse should be stopped. The most effective way to stop rankism is to achieve the support of those in power. The Persuader knows not all those with higher rank misuse their position. If those with influence necessary to bring about changes are committed to do so, the Persuader's job is much easier. Unfortunately, it sometimes takes a variety of persuasive techniques to capture the attention of those in charge.

That being the case, the Persuader may appeal to individuals who have been targets of abuse or who have witnessed rankism. It is possible that other members of a family, work, or political organization do not sanction rankism, even if it is not always clearly defined. There are strategies available to the Persuader to bring both Somebodies and Nobodies together in order to create an improved situation. Think of some contemporary Persuaders who convinced others that abuses were wrong. Mahatma Gandhi, Martin Luther King, Jr., Mother Theresa, and Nelson Mandella all worked with both the powerful and the downtrodden. They convinced those on top that systems of abuse were wrong. They also showed those who were exploited how to fight for their rights.

The Persuader does not pit one group against another. Rather, the Persuader works to convince people that rank abuse is unacceptable and can be stopped.

*Activist.* In 1982, Cindi Lamb and Candace Lightner brought together women from four states to create the beginnings of the largest victims' organization in the world. Both had lost children to a drunk driver. Mothers Against Drunk Driving (MADD) has grown to more than three million members with over six hundred chapters in eight countries. Besides helping to reduce the number of alcohol-related traffic fatalities and underage drinking, MADD has increased public awareness of responsible driving habits and encouraged legislation that holds drivers responsible for their behavior on the road. MADD estimates that one hundred and thirty-eight thousand people are alive today and many more targets assisted because of MADD's efforts.[5]

---

### ACTIVIST

| | |
|---|---|
| Behaviors: | Group organizer, media savvy, networking skills, knowledgeable |
| Emotions: | Committed, confident, brave, respectful |
| Typical line: | "Join us. We can make a difference." |
| Expects others to: | See the problem, donate time and talent |
| Response of targets: | Excited, hopeful, hard working |

---

The Activist is another example of right-rank. Activists use social organizations as means of dealing with rank abuse. That may mean bringing together targets of rank abuse to form a campaign or class action, perhaps working on educational and public awareness programs. In other words, bringing together groups of people who agree that rankism is a form of discrimination that social and legal systems should not accept.

Susan B. Anthony was an amazing activist. She created numerous organizations, each dedicated to the eradication of a specific abuse. She brought people together to promote abolition with the American Anti-Slavery Society and the Women's National Loyal League. She organized women to fight for their own labor rights through the Workingwomen's Central Association. She forged coalitions for suffrage through the American Equal Rights Association. Besides the many organizations she created, Anthony joined existing groups that worked to promote better education and women's personal and legal rights.

### Covert Nobody Rankists

Some Nobodies respond to rank abuse in ways that are subtler, more difficult to observe and identify. Covert Nobody Rankists may feel they show strength, but they misunderstand the nature of violence. American philosopher and writer Ralph Waldo Emerson said, "All violence...is not power but the absence of power." These Covert Nobody Rankists can be violent, but in ways that others may find difficult to detect. They also may abet assaults by others.

*Avenger.* Assisted by members of the al-Aqsa Martyrs Brigades, Ayat al-Akhras, an eighteen-year-old Palestinian girl, strapped on a belt of explosives and detonated it in a market, killing herself and a seventeen-year-old Israeli girl.

Her family members, who deplored her act of suicide, told of Ayat's increased anger with Arab leaders who did not take a stand against Israeli troops who had killed three cousins, a family friend, and a neighbor. Her brother had also been wounded. Her cousin, Mutlak Qassas, said Ayat had lost hope and wanted to send a message.[6]

---

**AVENGER**

| | |
|---|---|
| Behaviors: | Outsider, injured by a Somebody, wants a Somebody to lose, plans revenge |
| Emotions: | Hatred, depression, lack of empathy, impulsive |
| Typical line: | "I don't care if I win, so long as that Somebody loses." |
| Expects others to: | Be badly hurt or destroyed |
| Response of targets: | Anger, strike back hard and fast |

---

The Avenger creates deceptive plans to undermine the rankist by striking in unexpected areas. The rankist will know something has happened—vandalism, sabotage, violence—even war. Who caused this, and for what reason, may be less clear. This is why political terrorists are so effective and it is so difficult to know how to defend ourselves against them.

Avengers exist wherever offended Nobodies calculate that open retaliation would be harmful to them. Judith told me a story of a male friend to whom she agreed to rent a home. At the time, they were romantically involved. He agreed to make direct mortgage payments, rather than pay Judith, who usually sent the money. As she said, it made sense then, but it was not a wise decision. When they were no longer involved romantically, he began to miss mortgage payments. Then he put her house up for sale. How fortunate the title company closing the sale transaction found her name on the deed and she received her money. She was convinced that he had planned to take the money and leave town—because she had broken off their romantic involvement.

*Gossip.* An Internet website called "Grant Street 1999" caught the attention of many in Pittsburgh. Someone, who knew all the dirty little stories of those in the political system, was spreading tales about judges, campaign managers, and candidates. Someone was dispersing awkward details and naming names.

"I just got fed up," said the anonymous author.

As you may guess, those in power moved swiftly to shut down the site before they themselves were exposed.[7]

---

### GOSSIP

| | |
|---|---|
| Behaviors: | Secretive, poor interpersonal skills |
| Emotions: | Fears face-to-face confrontation, insecure, wishes to be seen as shrewd and knowing |
| Typical line: | "Know what I heard about _____?" |
| Expects others to: | Believe the stories, turn against the target |
| Response of targets: | Baffled, unsure, cynical |

---

A powerful way to undermine someone is to spread uncomplimentary stories. The tales may or may not be true. The truth of the story could be important if the perpetrator ended up in court on charges of defamation of character. That seldom happens. Whether true or not, gossip robs another person of dignity and the right to privacy.

The "facts" may be partly true or straight from someone's imagination. The problem is that gossip is never presented as fiction. Public personalities who are grist for the rumor mill must endure exposure, exaggeration, and out right lies about them. Sometimes, gossip can harm personal lives and careers of these individuals.

For private persons, gossip is always devastating. If you were a teenager and found that classmates were logging onto a website where they spread rumors about you, how would you feel? If you were one of the teachers attacked by those unidentified students, how would you react?[8]

*Placater.* Noreen just wanted everything to be peaceful at home. She knew Jake was a take-charge person when she married him, but it was a few months before she realized he expected to oversee her every move. It is because he loves me, she told herself, that he wants to know my schedule before he leaves home. It is love that drives him to call me half a dozen times during the day, to come home to check on me.

When Noreen met a friend for a spontaneous lunch, Jake screamed at her. He was shaking when he said, "I thought you'd been kidnapped. Someone took you away and killed you. Don't ever do that again!"

So, Noreen was careful. For three more years, she planned each daily event, told Jake where she would be and never overstayed her time. Three years, and Noreen lost her ability to function. Jake would come home and find her still in bed, not showered, and not dressed. Rather than be concerned, Jake seemed happier as Noreen gave up hope.

---

### PLACATER

| | |
|---|---|
| Behaviors: | Seeks harmony at any cost, presses others to agree with Somebodies, never questions |
| Emotions: | Fears disagreement, seeks protection |
| Typical line: | "Why can't we all just get along." |
| Expects others to: | Do whatever is necessary to keep the peace. |
| Response of targets: | Stifled, disrespected |

---

The Placater wants peace at any cost. Despite the personal cost to oneself or others, the Placater asks, "Can't we all just get along?" Willing to do and asking others to do whatever is necessary for peace, the Placater hopes everyone will be less angry and more agreeable.

Attempts at peace sometimes are commendable. The problem is that unending conciliatory behavior does not represent true feelings of the pacifist. Giving in on everything does not move peace forward, and often one side is placated at the expense of another.

All rank abusers benefit from the Placater's inaction. Noreen's own rankism enabled Jake to continue his rankism. Placaters fear disagreement and can survive only if they screw up their courage. In order to improve things, rankists and the systems that support them need to be exposed.

*Noble Sufferer.* It is a story about a small boy who was ill. When a visitor asked the boy if he wanted to get better, the child said no. He had misbehaved before he was ill and would do so again. The boy figured it was better he stay sick. The storyteller exclaimed over how wondrous the child's nature was.

Since the visitor talked to the child about regaining his health, I assume there was a good prognosis and I disagree with the narrator who applauded the child's answer. Someone taught that youngster to be a Noble Sufferer. He would have done better, I think, to have dealt with his illness and both hope and work for a healthy future. He certainly did not deserve to be ill because he misbehaved.

---

**NOBLE SUFFERER**

| | |
|---|---|
| Behaviors: | Weepy, whiney, lots of heavy sighing, limp |
| Emotions: | Worried about own health, wants attention, self-pitying, enjoys own suffering |
| Typical line: | "Only the Blessed suffer as I do." |
| Expects others to: | Sympathize, marvel at sanctified agony, give up their lives to provide care |
| Response of targets: | Irritated, manipulated, suffocated, angry |

---

For those who willingly accept their pain and discomfort, we offer support, even acclaim. Sainthood, a part of our tradition, is reserved for those who maintain a hopeful and lofty spirit despite their afflictions. Religious figures offer suggestions for how to manage such difficult times.

The Buddha's first Truth of Life is "dukkha" (suffering). He created a Path to help others move past suffering and the plan requires a person to accept responsibility for one's change, not expect others to do the work.

When our hardships cannot be alleviated, as with terminal illness or painful loss, we deserve to be seen as brave and lofty. It does not make sense, however, to encourage or applaud those who insist that suffering is a requirement for a meaningful life.

Sometimes, individuals confuse authentic sainthood with a fabricated version. The Noble Sufferer chooses not to change a painful situation brought on by Somebody Rankists. Instead, the Noble Sufferer seeks pity, even admiration, as a long-suffering victim. The dynamics of a Noble Sufferer are far more complicated than a discussion here might fully explain. Some humans, just as some birds or canines, not only accept domination by others, but even prefer it. Perhaps, Noble Sufferers experience pain, especially verbal haranguing, as proof that they have been noticed. Humiliation for the Noble Sufferer may mean approval and acceptance. The trouble is that rather than contribute to their own and others' flourishing life, Noble Sufferers hurt themselves, others, and the system. Noble Sufferers are rankists.

*Onlooker.* For at least three generations, Ray's family belonged to the same church. He was a preteen when he began to feel uneasy about some of the church's practices. His parents realized that Ray's best friend, Sam, attended a "competitor" church and told their son the friendship was over. Sam, they decided, was a bad influence.

"We're good kids," pleaded Ray, but to no avail.

When Ray's cousin got into trouble, the clergyman denounced her, and the family shunned her. His cousin had no choice but to leave town.

Yet, Ray could not imagine life without his church. He attended services, but with diminished enthusiasm. The few times he tried to discuss his misgivings, his family would hear none of it. He noticed that others his age were content and happy with the church, and he figured something was wrong with him.

Therefore, Ray learned to sit very quietly at church and at home. No one seemed to notice that he felt like an outsider.

### ONLOOKER

| | |
|---|---|
| Behaviors: | Sits on sidelines, doesn't participate, doesn't contribute |
| Emotions: | Wants to stay safe, can not leave and will not get involved, hopes others will do everything |
| Typical line: | "I'll just stay right here and watch." |
| Expects others to: | Show sympathy, affection, caring |
| Response of targets: | Pity, impatience, exasperation |

The Onlooker ceases participation within the group, moves to the periphery, but does not physically leave. Sociologist Robert Merton wrote about people who could not coordinate their goals and the means by which they would reach them. Where a Somebody Rankist is making life miserable, a Nobody may choose to stay, but stop participating.[9]

Sometimes, the wisest action is to leave. When Onlookers cannot envision another world, they may decide it is easier to stay and be very quiet.

Onlookers quit expressing their ideas, feelings, goals, and concerns. Their response is to relinquish their sense of self. They hope to save themselves by not disagreeing with the powers that be, but Onlookers can do themselves harm by becoming isolated. For example, rather than press the Gatekeepers for access to necessary commodities, they end up deprived and contributing to their own failure.

## Chapter Summary

Ways to immediately label Nobody types were posted in boxes beneath each illustration. *Overt* Nobody Rankists who are opposed to Somebody Rankists choose tactics that are more easily observed. They include:

- Retaliator, who slams back in the same way in which he or she was assaulted by a Somebody Rankist.
- Dog-Kicker, who strikes at someone more vulnerable rather than at the original Somebody Rankist; and
- Flatterer, who compliments Somebody Rankists in order to keep in good stead.

*Right-rank types* of overt responders use techniques that stop rankism. They respect all individuals involved and seek to improve relations with everyone. Two right-rank types are the:

- Persuader, who takes the case against rankist activities to those in power and asks that changes be made so everyone is treated with respect, and the
- Activist, who brings together those who agree that rank abuse is happening so they can organize to bring about change.

*Covert* Nobody Rankists use less obvious, more hidden ways to get back at the Somebody Rankists or aid rankist activities. Covert Omega Rankists are the:

- Avenger, who plans and executes a secret plan to get back at Somebody rankists without the Avenger being recognized;
- Gossiper, who spreads stories that undermine the Somebody Rankists;
- Placater, who, despite feeling otherwise, always gives, in hoping that everyone will get along;
- Noble Sufferer, who would rather be seen as enduring the pain of Somebody Rankists than acting to change the situation; and
- Onlooker, who does not leave the environment, but also does not partake of activities.

Does much of this sound familiar? Do you identify some of these types among these in your life? Chapter Eight will pull together both Somebody and Nobody Rankist types so you can see how others—and perhaps you—stack up. This will take you more deeply into what constitutes each Somebody and Nobody type. We are moving closer to right-rank.

**Reaching for Right-Rank: Nobody Rankists You Know**

1. Think of the Retaliator, a Dog-Kicker, and a Flatterer. Who do you know that embodies the traits of each?
2. Who do you know who might be a Persuader or an Activist?
3. Who is an Avenger you have known? Gossip? Placater? Noble Sufferer? Onlooker?

## CHAPTER EIGHT

# *Know Thyself: Find Your Place on the Battle Line*

Now that you know about rankism and some types of rankists, you are ready to find your place in the hierarchy line. Ways we each deal with conflict and threat are the basis of rankist types, as well as types of right-rank. As you study this chapter, you may want to review Chapters Six and Seven to refresh your understanding of the Somebody and Nobody types.

The two previous chapters depicted types that empha-sized extreme behavior. By using those dramatic examples, I hoped to help you recognize each type. On closer study, you may notice that types include a range from slight to drastic behaviors. In this chapter, I offer a broader view of types. Next, I discuss what you can learn from the survey information. Finally, you have an opportunity to score the Rank Conflict Inventory you took in Chapter Three. Here is your opportunity to decide your place in the Rankism lineup. When I undertake this sort of activity, I remember Shakespeare's works from his play *Hamlet*.

> *This above all: to thine own self be true,*
> *And it must follow, as the night the day,*
> *Thou canst not be false to any man.*

## A Broader View of Types

Types demonstrate opportunities for extreme rankism and for right-rank. If we adopt a type, we may sometimes exercise extreme behavior in that direction. Keep in mind that for each type, there is the potential for more moderate manifestations. We may act upon either the strengths or the weaknesses of that type. Listed below are some particulars.

*Somebody Rankists*

*Tyrants* can be credited for being committed to something larger than themselves. Their goals are clear, but their means can be questionable. Most of all, Tyrants do not trust others.

*Seething Giants* may be good leaders and dedicated members. They suffer from poor impulse control in that they just explode whenever they are threatened. This pushes people away from them.

*Gangsters* are good at recognizing those who are not contributing as they might. Gangsters may also be efficient, even to the extent that they want a fast resolution to a problem in order to get back to "important" things. Their flaw is they set up others to do their dirty work. All this shows a lack of respect for individuals and social groups.

*Sovereigns* are aware of danger and especially good at security measures. They can arrange the elements of safety. In so doing, they may oppress others and deny them their constitutional rights.

*Grandees* may have exceptional talents and know how to present themselves with impressive style. They also overstate their own importance and show a lack of regard for others' contributions.

*Extortionists*, who are sometimes mentors, may have high aptitudes and good mentoring skills. Their problem is that they are self-absorbed and want to take from others things to which they are not entitled.

*Scapegoaters* may have shown leadership in a variety ways, including having good ideas and knowing how to get things done. Their weakness is that they refuse to accept responsibility for their mistakes, so they blame those who are unable to protect themselves.

*Fabricators* are especially good at understanding systems that collect products or information and distribute them to those who can use it and benefit from them. The problem is that Fabricators may want to excel beyond their present expertise and not want to credit those who help them.

*Gatekeepers* understand how the system is constructed, so nothing works except through them. They likely are well organized in keeping people and things in their place. Problems occur when Gatekeepers prohibit those who have right to access because this hurts the entire system, as well as the individuals.

*Snubbers* may actually be quite capable and they may be effective with some individuals, usually those at their same

level or higher up the ladder. Snubbers deal with their inse-
curity by staying separate of those with whom they are not
comfortable. Snubbers choose to ignore anyone who makes
them uneasy.

### Nobody Rankists

*Retaliators* are quick to recognize a variety of styles and
they have a sense, however crude, of justice. Retaliators, however, think of justice as getting even. They do not consider
other forms of justice.

*Dog-Kickers* are individuals who have experienced abuse
from an Somebody Rankists. At some level, they know they
are both Somebody and Nobody. Dog-Kickers, however,
ignore the source of their pain. They hurt others instead, and
without realizing that they are now acting the same as the
Somebody Rankist who hurt them.

*Flatterers* could have written part of this section. They want
to find the good in everyone, and they encourage others to
succeed. Flatterers want to ensure that Somebody Rankists
continue to protect them, so sometimes their compliments
are less than genuine.

### Right-Rank Types

*Persuaders* are skilled at human relations and care about
the individuals involved in conflicts. Sometimes, however,
Persuaders can be so enamored with the techniques of persuasion they forget persuasion is just their way to bring
people to agreement. Instead their methods become ways to
empower themselves.

*Activists* work with groups and have learned to accomplish
things with a cluster of individuals by both leading and following. It is possible for Activists to be so carried away with

the cause that they forget about the individuals involved. Sometimes Activists can see the world in terms of those who are for us and those who are against us.

*More Nobody Rankists*

*Avengers* are passionately committed to their cause and are capable planners. They are not willing to deal with problems out front where those involved may negotiate an agreement. Rather, they have no qualms harming those who are not part of the conflict.

*Gossips* are very tuned into what it going on and how people are dealing with one another. Sometimes, they distort events to be more like a soap opera than real life, but they do study human dynamics. Gossips do not distinguish facts from lies, and they avoid facing the people about whom they spread rumors.

*Placaters* genuinely care about people. They sincerely want people to live together in peace. They tend to ignore reality and ignore problems, and are timid about making changes to improve things.

*Noble Sufferers*, unlike some types, are aware of feelings. They may even notice signs of others' pain. Rather than take action against rankism, Noble Sufferers use their ploys to get attention for themselves. They may even relish their lowly position.

*Onlookers* are observers and may recognize aspects of conflict situations that no one else notices. Their position offers them insights that could help the situation. Though they have much to offer, they elect to stay apart and may not want to contribute to bettering things.

Below is a chart that offers a brief summary of some broad, core components of each type.

## Some Core Components for Types

| Type | Strength | Weakness |
|---|---|---|
| **Somebody Rankists** | | |
| Tyrant | Committed; goals clear | Means can be questionable; lacks confidence in others |
| Seething Giant | Could be leader; may be dedicated | Poor impulse control; pushes people away |
| Gangster | Recognizes problems; could be efficient | Manipulates others; does not respect individual rights |
| Sovereign | Strong on security; Good organizer | Oppresses others; prevents free expression |
| Grandee | May be talented; possibly elegant | Overstates own importance; lacks regard for others |
| Extortionist | May have mentor skills; aptitudes | Selfish; treats others as puppets, not humans |
| Scapegoater | May have leadership skills; may have good ideas | Does not accept responsibility for own failings; blames the weak and defenseless |
| Fabricator | Knows systems; energetic worker | Wants to excel beyond own expertise; does not credit others |
| Gatekeeper | Knows system; well organized | Prevents others from rightful access; preferential treatment hurts system |
| Snubber | May have skills; might be good with some people | Stays separate; ignores certain individuals |
| **Nobody Rankists** | | |
| Retaliator | Knows several styles; cares passionately | Set on getting even; may not consider alternate options |
| Dog-Kicker | Knows rank abuse; knows Somebody and Nobody rankists | Ignores source of pain; unaware of displaced anger |
| Flatterer | Sees good in all; wants others to succeed | Seeks protection from those stronger; sometimes untruthful |

## Some Core Components for Types *(continued)*

| Type | Strength | Weakness |
|------|----------|----------|
| *Right-Rank Types* | | |
| Persuader | Human relations skills; cares for people | Could be smitten with process; could lose track of goal |
| Activist | Good group skills; willing to both lead and follow | Cause could be more important than individuals; either with us or against us |
| *More Nobody Rankists* | | |
| Avenger | Capable planner; passionately committed | Refuses to be above board; willing to strike those not involved |
| Gossip | Aware of human dynamics; knows what is happening | Does not separate facts from lies; unwilling to personally confront others |
| Placater | Cares about people; wants peace | Tends to ignore reality; unwilling to take chances |
| Noble Sufferer | Aware of feelings: may notice others' pain | Seeks attention for self; may enjoy lowly position |
| Onlooker | Notices much; may have insights others lack | Keeps self apart; does not contribute |

## Learning from the Rank Conflict Inventory

The only reason for taking the Rank Conflict Inventory is to help move yourself toward right-rank so you can stop rankism in your life. If you can accomplish right-rank without taking this self-inventory, that is fine.

As you prepare to score your Rank Conflict Inventory, here are some things to keep in mind.

1. A self-inventory is just one way to organize materials so it makes sense to us. Consider how the information you learn may offer a different way to understand yourself.

The challenge is to be honest with yourself. Never let a self-inventory convince you of something you know is untrue.

2.  The types we select are ways you judged how you might react in hierarchy conflicts. They offer you clues about how you might overdo any of them and become rankists.

### Reaching for Right-Rank: Score the Rank Conflict Inventory

You may choose to score your survey without sharing it with others. That is your prerogative. The important things are to be honest with yourself when you take the survey and to learn from the results.

1.  Score your answers on the Rank Conflict Inventory from the end of Chapter Three.

    - In the quadrangle, below, the ten types are listed in each category: Overt Somebodies, Overt Nobodies, Covert Somebodies, and Covert Nobodies. After each type are listed the three items on the Rank Conflict Inventory that are associated with that particular type.

    - ON A SEPARATE PIECE OF PAPER, list each type for which you selected an item in the Chapter Three exercise. For example, if you selected item number 1, write down Tyrant. Then, if you selected number 5, write down Grandee.

    - If you selected any type more than once, indicate how many times.

    - In the Inventory, there are six groups, and you were asked to select two answers in each group. If you selected each type once, your list will include twelve types, the highest number of types possible. The lowest number of types you can pick is four, and each of those would be selected three times.

## Rank Conflict Inventory Items by Types

Overt

| | |
|---|---|
| Tyrant: 1, 16, 25 | Retaliator: 3, 40, 48 |
| Seething Giant: 2, 18, 29 | Dog Kicker: 7, 39, 42 |
| Gangster: 8, 17, 30 | Flatterer: 9, 31, 50 |
| Sovereign: 6, 14, 24 | Persuader: 4, 34, 47 |
| Grandee: 5, 11, 27 | Activist: 10, 36, 45 |

Somebodies ———————————————— Nobodies

| | |
|---|---|
| Extortionist: 26, 49, 51 | Avenger: 12, 35, 57 |
| Scapegoater: 21, 43, 58 | Gossip: 13, 38, 52 |
| Fabricator: 28, 44, 53 | Placater: 15, 32, 59 |
| Gatekeeper: 23, 41, 60 | Noble Sufferer: 19, 33, 55 |
| Snubber: 22, 46, 56 | Onlooker: 20, 37, 54 |

Covert

- The more types your choices fell under, the larger your repertoire of responses to threatening situations.

- The number of items chosen within each quadrangle is an indication of the classes of rankism you tend to use. For example, if you select mostly Overt Somebody items, you may be openly domineering toward those beneath you in a hierarchy. If you chose mostly Covert Somebody items, you could be quietly combative toward those below you. If your largest number of items comes from the Nobody Overt quadrangle you may be visibly contentious toward those above you. If your highest number of items falls under Nobody Covert, you may be unobtrusively militant toward those above you.

- If most of the items are above the dividing line, your quarrelsome behavior with those both above or below you is right out in front of everyone. If most items are below the line, you are more likely to fight back in the shadows.
- For each type you selected on the "Rank Conflict Inventory," come up with some examples of how you have used conflict techniques in your life to deal with hierarchy conflicts. Remember, there is no one right profile for the items you choose. The idea is to learn about types of responses you use, and how they can be rankist.

**Chapter Summary**

We looked at types in a broader perspective—to see what strengths and weaknesses each offer. If you took and scored the Rank Conflict Inventory, I hope you have a better understanding of how you function in a stressful hierarchy. The next chapter will give you more information that takes types deeper. It is a further way to understand various rankist types, and will take you closer to right-rank.

## Part Four

# Organize to Stop Rankism

Blend fear with the will to power and you have the makings of rankism. Karen Horney (about whom you will learn more in Chapter Nine) wrote, "The quest for power is…a protection against helplessness and against insignificance."[1] The dynamics for both Somebody Rankists and Nobody Rankists are the same. We may think Somebody Rankists are more assured and self-confident, but the opposite is true. Those who are self-assured do not treat others poorly. Both

Somebody Rankists and Nobody Rankists are terrified of having too little control.

Chapter Nine begins by describing what it is that each rankist type fears. Chapters Nine and Ten will also discuss the following:

*Conflict Postures.* When any of us enters a battle between Somebodies and Nobodies, we assume a posture. By understanding your own and the rankist's conflict posture, you can better prepare to stop rankism in your life.

*Takers, Receivers, and Givers.* To better understand the type of rankist you are dealing with, you will learn to recognize whether they are takers or givers in this world. Takers grasp what they want without concern for others' rights; givers bestow on others those things the other person may need. You will also learn to recognize those who passively wait to be served by others—the receivers.

*Specific Rankist Situations.* As you prepare to do battle against rankists, you will want to identify and/or better understand the dynamics of the rankism in your specific situation—whether that is at school, in the workplace, within your family, relationships, or community. I will point to lots of places where you can learn more about rankism in each of these categories.

*Effects of Rankism.* In order to successfully engage in this battle, you will also want to recognize the physical, emotional, and psychological effects that rankism can have on yourself and others.

*Proposed Changes.* What changes will you aim for? Do you want changes in behavior, structure, or attitude? You decide.

*Battle Plan.* Now that you are ready to initiate your battle for right-rank, there are several courses of action you can take: a series of proactive steps, a talk directly with a rankist, and a discussion with someone who can influence a change. If none of these plans works, you may decide to take on activism.

## CHAPTER NINE

# Big Picture: Conflict Strategies against Rankism

Kurt Lewin is purported to have said, "If you want truly to understand something, try to change it." To really comprehend rankism, we must be change-makers. So far, you have looked at the problem of rankism as set forth in the first eight chapters. Next comes a strategy, a perspective from which you will create an action plan. In the final chapter, I will show you how to formulate plans that can stop rankism.

Strategy grows from a reflection of behaviors that do and do not work in hostile situations. Now that you know more about yourself, you are prepared to look more deeply into what constitutes a rankist. In the following discussion, I will explain how rankists are alike and how they are different. With this information, we will create strategies for eliminating rankism.

Just as fear is an important component in creating rankism, so fear is important to stopping rankism. That is because rankist types share certain specific fears. Further, more than one Somebody Rankist and Nobody Rankist share certain features with one or another rankist type. Several Somebodies and Nobodies have similar postures toward adversaries. Finally, various Somebodies and Nobodies show parallel tendencies toward bettering communities.

## What Each Type Fears Most

In order to surpass others, both Somebody Rankists and Nobody Rankists work to maintain or increase their power within the hierarchy. That is not unusual, since we all pursue goals to improve our place in life. What makes rankists unique is their abuse of others, abuse that stems from a fear that Alfred Adler described:

> Behind everyone who behaves as if he were superior to others, we can suspect a feeling of inferiority that calls for very special efforts of concealment. It is as if a man feared that he was too small and walked on his toes to make himself seem taller.[1]

These distinctive fears manifest themselves with both rankist types and right-rank types. If you want to assume a right-rank position, you would do well to understand the fears that come with it. Social philosopher Eric Hoffer advised us: "You can discover what your enemy fears most by observing the means he [or she] uses to frighten you." For each type, the ways in which he or she tries to instill—or deal with—fear tell us what the person fears the most.

*Somebody Types – Overt and Covert*

**Tyrant.** Tyrants dread being intimidated, oppressed, or controlled. They worry that someone will be smarter or more talented than they. Someone may notice the Tyrant's mistakes. Because they fear anyone who is unpredictable or self-expressive, Tyrants hold a tight rein on everyone they consider beneath them.

**Seething Giant.** Seething Giants are as terrified of their own fury as are their targets. Their outbursts cover a dread that they are unable to meet the requirements of the situation. Consequently, Seething Giants use their anger as a weapon to keep others in place.

**Gangster.** Gangsters fear being pushed aside. For a variety of reasons, they are unable to deal with certain individuals, and that lack of human skill puts the Gangster's position at risk. Getting others to share responsibility for banishing the target helps ensure the Gangster's place in the group.

**Sovereign.** Sovereigns dread that they are not really inspired (or perhaps, not even divinely chosen) leaders. Maybe those who would betray the Sovereign are but a few who know the truth. That is why Sovereign types demand absolute loyalty.

**Grandee.** Grandees worry that they may be just another member of humanity, rather than someone very, very special. They surround themselves with objects and events where they can be the major player. Without others making a fuss over them, Grandees fear they will be nothing.

**Extortionist.** Extortionists fear they are unworthy of respect, unable to perform, and that others will not care for or be attached to them. Rather than strive for love and respect, Extortionists force others to meet their needs. In so doing, the Extortionist treats others as objects, not living human beings.

*Scapegoater.* Scapegoaters anguish about looking bad. If others realize they were wrong, Scapegoaters may not survive. It is better that someone else accepts responsibility for their shortcomings.

*Fabricator.* Fabricators are concerned that they cannot meet others' expectations. They fear being exposed as frauds. As a result, they pass off as their own works and possessions that belong to others.

*Gatekeeper.* Gatekeepers worry that the group will not need them. They could lose everything if others found a way to function without them. To protect their position, Gatekeepers guard access to people and supplies others need in order to function well.

*Snubber.* Snubbers panic at the prospect of being rejected. They would rather ignore someone than take the chance of being discounted. When Snubbers ignore others, they make sure those persons know they are now Nobodies.

### Nobody Types – Overt

*Retaliator.* Retaliators fear that someone will be stronger than they. If others take advantage of them, Retaliators dread their loss of freedom. As if it will keep them safe, a Retaliator reacts quickly against a Somebody Rankist by using the same tactics as that rankist.

*Dog-Kicker.* Dog-Kickers are so afraid of misplaced strikes, they forget where the abuse they felt originally came from. In their muddled fear, Dog-Kickers lose track of who is friend and who is foe, and they end up striking out at someone who never harmed them.

*Flatterer.* Flatterers fear being alone. If they are outside the realm of protection, Flatters may have to stand up for themselves. In their desperation, Flatterers will "kiss up" to anyone in power.

### Right-Rank Types

*Persuader.* Persuaders worry that their efforts will not be enough. If they cannot find a way to bring together those in conflict, the same bad things will continue to happen. So the Persuader uses every available opportunity to appeal his or her case to those who can make a difference.

*Activist.* Activists dread the prospect that their group will not work well enough. If the strategies and plans they devise will be ineffective, they fear that extreme measures could be taken by those on all sides. Thus, Activists may continually look for ways to improve the working relationships within any group.

### Nobody Types – Covert

*Avenger.* Avengers are scared of face-to-face confrontation. They also worry that their plan will not work or that they will be caught. So, they secretly devise schemes to attack Somebody Rankists from a distance.

*Gossip.* Gossips fear they will be publicly disgraced. Yet, they also fear direct encounters with those they charge. Once they begin to spread rumors, Gossips worry they will be exposed, be asked to "prove" what they said.

*Placater.* Placaters shudder at open discord. Disagreements may lead to change. Change is terrifying for Placaters, who fear they may lose their comfortable position within the group. Consequently, they refuse to take a stand against rankism and encourage others to do the same.

*Noble Sufferer.* Noble Sufferers fear losing their unique role as victim. If someone were to suggest that everyone has problems, the Noble Sufferer would be ordinary. That could mean Noble Sufferers would need to find better ways to deal with their pain than merely seeking sympathy.

*Onlooker.* Onlookers worry that they can take no effective part in the group's activities. They fear that someone will notice they are awkward and unsure, and they do not trust that they could do well elsewhere. Thus, the Onlooker stays in an uncomfortable situation and observes from the sidelines, rather than try to move against rankism.

## Conflict Postures

In a threatening environment, we orient ourselves with respect to those who may attack us. The posture we assume tells how we are dealing with the situation. Karen Horney, who studied human behavior, was interested in how we cope in a hostile world.[2] She offered three ordinations or stances we may take when threatened. We are *compliant* when we move toward those who threaten us. We are *detached* when we move away. We are *aggressive* when we move against those who cause us concern. She offered an in-depth study of her three conflict ordinations. I propose a fourth, an *integrative* conflict posture used by someone who moves among conflict participants.

*Compliant.* According to Horney, those who move toward the opposition comply with whatever others demand. When compliant, one wants approval, belonging, and love. Those who move toward the opposition appreciate individuals who are nice, unselfish, generous, and humble. They are subservient to others and disapprove of anyone who wields power. This means those who are compliant cuddle up to people they despise.[3]

*Detached.* Horney described those who move away as detached. Detached individuals avoid emotional involvement.

They deny needing others or feeling attached to anyone. Those who are detached are proud of their ability to be self-sufficient, independent, and unique, and tend to be secretive and nonconformist. They depend on their intellect to surpass the knowledge and organizing skills of everyone else. By being separate from others, detached persons are also estranged from themselves and their own emotions.[4]

*Aggressive.* Those who move against their adversaries, wrote Horney, are aggressive. Aggressive persons assume that everyone is an enemy and the only way to survive is to be tough and take charge. They never admit or show their fear and are firmly unsentimental realists and strategists.

Those who are aggressive aim to be the best and strongest and are always right. They prize their own fighting spirit and are bad losers. Aggressive individuals hide behind a variety of behaviors in order to take control. Their techniques depend on their talents, but they are sure to make careful plans, use others, and possibly abuse those with lesser power.[5]

*Integrative.* To Horney's three conflict ordinations, I add one more: the person who moves among those in strife in order to integrate everyone. Rather than accept a hostile environment, those who integrate ply skills to change the situation. They are assertive, not aggressive. They are independent, but not separate from others. Those who integrate are active, rather than dependent; affirming, rather than helpless.

The "Postures in Conflict Strategies" chart below compares conflict postures with public exposure. How do we stand in relation to others in a conflict situation, and are we overt or covert in our actions? Each of the rankist types falls somewhere on this chart. By looking at the types this way, we gain some understanding of which Somebody and which Nobody types share similar orientations in a hostile world

Somebody Rankists and Nobody Rankists are more alike than they may sometimes appear.

## Postures in Conflict Strategies

| Postures | Exposure | |
|---|---|---|
| | Overt | Covert |
| Compliant (Moving Toward) | Nobody<br>Flatterer | Nobody<br>Noble Sufferer<br>Placater |
| Detached (Moving Away) | Somebody<br>Grandee | Somebody<br>Snubber<br><br>Nobody<br>Onlooker |
| Aggressive (Moving Against) | Somebody<br>Tyrant<br>Seething Giant<br>Gangster<br>Sovereign<br><br>Nobody<br>Retaliator<br>Dog-Kicker | Somebody<br>Extortionist<br>Scapegoater<br>Fabricator<br>Gatekeeper<br><br>Nobody<br>Avenger<br>Gossip |
| Integrative (Moving Among) | Nobody<br>Persuader<br>Activist | |

## Takers, Receivers, and Givers

*Social Concern.* Psychologist Alfred Adler[6] considered social concern, regard for one's community, to be crucial to our mental health. Those who are interested in giving to other members of society also gain much for themselves. Ask a hospital volunteer and you will hear about the personal rewards of doing for others.

*Amount of Activity.* In his discussion of the importance of social interest, Adler also included how much energy we put into social concern, the level of activity we expend toward projects that will improve society. There is a difference, thought Adler, between those who care about their family, business, and community, but contribute little, and persons who devote much of their time to these aspects of their lives. Levels of activity and social concern help us understand rankists' give-and-take with those around them. The chart below divides levels of social concern and degrees of activity into low or high. Types with high activity and low social concern expend their vigor on their own interests, for they are the takers in this world. Types with low activity, whether they have high or low levels of social concern, wait for others to take care of them and are the receivers among us. As with takers, the receivers are primarily interested in their own comfort. Types with high activity and high social concern are the givers. Those of right-rank care enough to be actively involved with anything that will make this a better world. Each of us can do our little part to contribute to that work.

## Takers, Givers, and Receivers

| Degree of Activity | Social Concern | |
|---|---|---|
| | High | Low |
| High | Nobody Givers<br>Persuader<br>Activist | Somebody Takers<br>Tyrant<br>Seething Giant<br>Gangster<br>Sovereign<br>Grandee<br>Extortionist<br>Scapegoater<br>Fabricator<br>Gatekeeper<br><br>Nobody Takers<br>Retaliator<br>Dog-Kicker<br>Avenger<br>Gossip |
| Low | Nobody Receivers<br>Flatterer<br>Placater | Somebody Receivers<br>Snubber<br><br>Nobody Receivers<br>Noble Sufferer<br>Onlooker |

**Chapter Summary**

The word *strategy* is usually associated with military. Though we are looking at situations of conflict, sometimes even leading to violence and war, use of weapons is no way to stop rankism. So, what sort of perspective will best suit us when creating plans to stop rankism?

First, we need to remember that the goal is to stop abuse. Stopping rankism will improve all our individual and shared lives. Thoughtless violence by rankists tears down individuals and works against an improved community. Therefore, we *cannot* use violence and degradation to accomplish our goal. If ever that dictum begins to wane, remember the example that Mahatma Gandhi set with his campaign of nonviolence.

Second, we need to use means that show we understand (a) how rankism works, (b) how rankist behavior can be identified, (3) what rankist types fear, (4) specific rankist postures, and (5) what degrees of activity and social concern help distinguish givers from takers and receivers.

One's rank can be used to exploit others and gain one's personal ends. Rank can also be used to respect others and to better the world. Always pay attention to the human community. As Alfred Adler wrote, "Everything we call a mistake shows a lack of social interest."[7]

In the last chapter, we will pull together plans for stopping rankism.

**Reaching for Right-Rank: Map Strategies for Rankists You Know**

Select one or more rankist types that remind you of someone you know who abuses rank. For each, map a strategy for dealing with them.

1.  Describe the behavior of the person that leads you to define him or her as a particular type of rankist. Be careful not to judge the person so much as to describe his or her behavior.

2.  List what you perceive that the rankist most fears, and see if you have some instances of where that fear may have shown through the rankist's armor.
3.  Describe the rankist's conflict posture. Try to recall a specific instance of how the rankist has demonstrated his or her ordination toward you or others?
4.  Given what you know of the rankist, how would you estimate his or her degree of activity and social concern.

CHAPTER TEN

# *The Context and Details: Breaking the Cycle of Rankism*

**R**emember the story of Karl from Chapters Six and Seven—the man who devoted twenty-eight years of his life to a company, only to be tossed out? Karl's immediate reaction was a desire to sabotage the plant, and then he decided to consider other possibilities. This chapter aims to help Karl and others to deal with rankism in their lives. This is where the rubber meets the road, or knuckles rap doors, or voices reach ears. Whatever the metaphor, we now prepare for action. I like to remember Margaret Mead's comment,

"Never doubt that a small group of thoughtful, committed citizens can change the world; indeed, it's the only thing that ever has."

In addition to recognizing the types of rankist behavior, anyone who wants to stop rankism needs to (1) identify the specific situation where rankism occurs, (2) recognize the effects of rankism, (3) detail what should be changed, and (4) decide on a course or courses of action—in other words, on a battle plan. At the back of the book, in the Notes for this chapter, you will find pages of resources that can take you further toward stopping rankism in your life.

## Identify the Specific Situation

In 1998, two men from Laramie, Wyoming, killed Matthew Shepard, a twenty-one-year-old student. They lured Shepard to a remote area where they tied him to a fence post, robbed and beat him. Theft, however, was not the motive. The men who perpetrated this crime admitted that they had killed Shepard because he was gay.

Although each of the killers were sentenced to life in prison for the murder, Matthew's family, and others who were so appalled by the circumstances of his death have become activists for public debate on homophobia and gay-bashing, two extreme forms of rankism. Federal hate crime legislation presently includes violent crimes against others because of their race, color, religion, or national origin. It does not include violent crimes against others because of their gender, sexuality, or disabilities. Whatever their specific context, rankists move to meet their personal needs while depriving others of their own. They treat humans as objects without concern for individual feelings or safety. Such rankism may occur at school, work, within the family, relationships, the community, and in any other situations in which particular individuals function in a specific organization for a definite purpose.

My purpose in discussing each of the following situations is to give you a broad overview and then suggest where you might learn more.

*Schools.* Most of us remember instances of rankism among youngsters with whom we attended school. No longer are we hearing that "Boys will be boys," or even "Girls will be girls." With the killing at Columbine High School in Colorado, the public became aware of the effects of school bullying. Cruelty to children is no longer acceptable. Teachers are trained to recognize and deal with rankism among classmates.[1] Stephanie Heuer asked students to complete the two lines, "I feel like a Nobody when _____," and "I feel like a Somebody when _____." She compiled their answers in an illustrated children's book.[2] For parents seeking ways to help children caught in such rankism, Heuer's book is a great introduction.[3]

About fifteen percent of elementary school children are bullied, and direct bullying increases until it reaches an apex in junior high school.[4] Two specific instances of rankism in schools can be found among adolescent girls and among youngsters in athletics. We are hearing more about instances of girls using rankist behavior.[5] Rachel Simmons described the covert behavior of girls who act as Gangster Rankist types.[6] Rosalind Wiseman went so far as to create names such as "Queen Bee," and "Target" to describe the dramas enacted by some teenage rankists.[7] Both boys and girls are susceptible to rankism in sports, and there are places to learn more about such abuse.[8]

The important thing to remember is that children are not born with an understanding of how to behave with others. They need to be taught that it is not okay to mistreat their schoolmates. Parents also need to consider how they mistreated others when they were in school. Perhaps, a boy's father was not bullied, but he did stand by while others were.

If children play any part in mistreatment of others, they need to be educated about their role and how to stop rankism. In other words, the adults must lead the way for their children against school rankism.

Do not forget that adults are also susceptible to rankism as they continue their education. Most post-secondary institutions have become sensitive to rankism and should be expected to respond to reports of abuse. Talk to an instructor or administrator if you incur or witness such mistreatment.

*Workplaces.* Denise enjoyed her consulting work. Her clients knew one another, and together they formed a Denise fan club. Clients agreed that she knew her stuff and was passionately committed to seeing them benefit and prosper from her work. Denise's only problem was the organization for which she worked.

She always received the highest ratings from her clients, and yet Denise's boss offered her no opportunity for advancement. Imagine how she felt when she inadvertently learned that he had once actually lowered her marks from clients and colleagues so he would not have to give her a wage increase.

Besides having a boss who was a Gatekeeper Rankist, Denise worked in an establishment designed to prevent promotions for any consultant. Worse yet, consultants had a no-competition clause in their contracts. To do her work outside this organization, Denise first would have to support herself in another profession for five years.

Adults spend at least one quarter of their time at work. Those hours can offer opportunities for growth and fulfillment, or they can be occasions of anguish. Mistreatment in the workplace is all too common and the human and production implications are substantial.[9]

Several good books will assist you to understand rankism in the work environment. If there are bullies at school, it is no surprise that there are also bullies at work. Tim Fields described the "Serial Bully," which is a compilation of rankist types. Fields' Internet site is an excellent source of information about abuse.[10] Chauncey Hare and Judith Ware used the term "work abuse" to describe both active instances of rankism, such as scapegoating and denial of due process, as well as rankism through neglect.[11]

One book worth looking at is *The Violence-Prone Workplace*. Richard Dennenberg and Mark Braverman looked at, not the individuals who are rankists, but at the work situation that can foster rankist violence.[12] Remember the example from Chapter Six about the Gangster Rankists? Employees were unwittingly part of a plan to turn against a colleague who was eventually fired. Noa Davenport and her colleagues compiled a fine book about "mobbing." They consider mobbing as harmful as physical assault or drug abuse. Because mobbing is not illegal in the United States, those who plan to prevent it need a clear understanding of how this brand of rankism works.[13]

Some authors provide specific pointers for dealing with rankism in the workplace. Kathleen Ryan and Daniel Oestreich described how a work environment becomes saturated with fear. They counsel managers about how to remove fear and regain employee trust.[14] Peter Block's book on empowerment is a classic on becoming a right-rank manager.[15]

Businesses that refuse to accept rankism do more than protect individuals. Businesses prosper when everyone is respected. Employees can benefit from looking at Samuel Culbert and John Ullman's suggestions to employees for creating good relations with their bosses.[16] Companies that prevent rankism can, according to Jim Collins, move from good to great.[17]

*Families.* Dramatic headlines attest to how awful rankism can be when it is found in the family. On June 20, 2001, Andrea

Yates drowned her five children. In December of that year, Christian Longo murdered his wife and three children. On April 23, 2003, David Brame, the Tacoma, Washington, chief of police, killed his wife, Crystal, and himself—while their children looked on. Previously, Crystal had reported his abuse and had been seeking a divorce.

Most instances of abuse resulting from rankism in the family never attract the attention of the media. There are numerous ways we regular folk can learn more about fear and misuse of power in the family. *Family Violence Across the Lifespan* is a comprehensive look at violence within families.[18] The insidious dynamic of youngsters raised in rankist families is they too often pass on rankism to their own children.[19] Most municipalities offer assistance for both the rankist and those abused. Social service agencies, law enforcement, medical centers, and other community services can work together to stop violent rankism in families.[20]

There is a lot of information available for individuals who struggle to survive family rankism. Steven Wolin described families besieged with rankism, as well as ways that family members can rebound.[21] Robert Becker detailed specific types within the dysfunctional family and ways to diagram one's own family.[22] Meg Dugan and Roger Hock offered helpful advice for women leaving abusive marriages.[23]

Please remember that dynamics are unique to each family. Sometimes only a professional can point out the ways in which rankism creeps in. This is someone from outside the family who is trained to recognize the subtleties of fear and misused power among members of a domestic unit. We usually cannot recognize the dysfunctional features of our own family. We are too close and too much a part of the action to have a clear perspective. To understand your own situation, consider taking your entire family to a family counselor. If not everyone is willing to go, take those who will. If only you are willing, go alone.

*Relationships.* One section of an adult day care center was the responsibility of a group that called themselves "The Team." For nearly a year, the three workers functioned as equals in that they shared scheduling, job distribution, paperwork and decision-making. They respected one another, and yet certain problems at the center continued to surface without ever being resolved. Part-time helpers and volunteers became so agitated that they finally took their concerns to the head administrator.

At a combined meeting, each group offered their views of what was wrong. The volunteers were discouraged because they believed "nothing will ever change." Upon reflection, the full-time workers realized that, indeed, a host of problems were never addressed because it took so long for the three of them to agree on everything.

"The Team" and their administrator decided that consensus was not the best way to make decisions. They selected one of their team to be lead member. At first, the change was awkward, but within six months everyone was actually working together much better.

Rankism can afflict a variety of personal relationships. Some, such as parent-child and employer-employee, are composed of formal rank differences. Relations among those of all different ranks is what this book is about.

Other relationships have implicit, more negotiable rank differences. The colleagues comprising "The Team" at the day care center had an equal and negotiable relationship. Like relationships include those of mates and friends. Informal contracts that bind "equal" individuals, those of the same rank, can be at least as complicated as those between members of different ranks. Sometimes equality, despite its appeal, does not work in a particular environment.

As we develop "equal" unions, we contract with one another. Usually, those contracts are negotiated with inordinate delicacy, and continually renegotiated. When I was first married, I intended to stay home when my children were born. While many women find fulfillment with full-time parenting, I was most unhappy away from the working world I had known. So, my husband and I renegotiated our roles and I went back to teaching. It was not always easy, but we somehow made the new agreement work.

*Friends.* If you know how to recognize them, clear stages exist by which we progress toward closer relationships. Two people move from stranger to acquaintance to casual friend to close friend. It is tricky to discern if both are moving in the same direction at the same rate. One person may introduce someone as "my friend." What if the other person does not regard the relationship as a friendship? Some consider anyone they know as a friend. Others reserve that term for those with whom they share personal ideas and feelings. If you make a list of those you consider friends, you can learn a lot about your own definition of "friend."

Seldom do friendships go untested. If something is wrong with the dynamics of your friendship, you can feel it, even if you are unable to state clearly what is wrong. While there can be other problems that impinge on a friendship, rankism can be the reason the relationship is not working. Jan Yager wrote a book that may help explain what is wrong with your friendship and help you decide whether to work at fixing the friendship.[24]

*Mates.* It is usually easier to slide away from a rankist friend than from a rankist mate. Even if not legally married, the interactions between lovers can be difficult to change. Sometimes, the rankist behavior in intimate relations is physically abusive.[25] Other rankists use verbal abuse.[26] To find ways to understand relations with rankist mates, women can easily locate books.[27] It is important to remember that men are also targets of rankism.[28] For both men and women caught in a rankist relationship, information is beneficial.[29]

If the couple is associated with children, the young people will be affected by anything that is wrong with the mates' relationship.

*Community.* Our towns and cities offer us innumerable opportunities to gather with others. We can choose from among recreation groups—such as, parks programs, team sports, or fitness clubs. We could gather with others to play bridge, attend athletic games, or support school arts events. We might select political involvement—e.g., working for political parties, candidates, and causes. We might pick service groups—including, Lions, Kiwanis, Rotary, Boys and Girls Clubs, Alcoholics Anonymous, Weight Watchers or Newcomers. We might favor professional organizations—Chamber of Commerce, Veterans of Foreign Wars, realtor groups, trial lawyers, contractors, or exchange clubs. We may be drawn to arts organizations, embracing theaters, symphonies, choruses, bands, or dance companies. On the other hand, many might opt for religious organizations.

Usually, we choose organizations that embody our interests, concerns, and beliefs. We expect these community groups to include people with whom we share much and who function to meet common goals. While innumerable community organizations do commendable work, some can include rankism.

When a service group spends time advancing its workers rather than altruistic goals, we have reason to be disgusted. When an arts group is more interested in profits than creative expression, we can become disappointed. When professional organizations direct more energy toward achieving political power than toward promoting the integrity of work or maintaining professional standards among its members, we can be outraged. When religious organizations protect their hierarchy, rather than their abused members, we can be disenchanted.

It is easy to just walk away from community organizations that become rankist. Usually, community groups go wrong because they forget their original goals or they subvert the collective good for personal profit. Consider if you care sufficiently about the group to work from within to attack and remove the rankism that infests it.

### Recognize the Effects of Rankism

The toll on individuals caught in the cycle of rankism is enormous. Here are partial lists of emotional, physical, and psychological reactions to various forms of rankism.

*Emotional Reactions*

| | |
|---|---|
| alienation | anger |
| anxiety | betrayal |
| chronic fear | disbelief |
| despair | emptiness |
| failure | grief |
| guilt | irritability |
| isolation | numbness |
| panic | regret |
| self-blame | self-doubt |
| self hatred | shame |
| suppressed anger | untrusting |
| vulnerability | worthlessness |

*Physical Reactions*

| | |
|---|---|
| appetite loss | asthma |
| bladder infections | chronic fatigue |
| cramps | headaches |
| heart palpitations | high blood pressure |
| insomnia | Irritable Bowel Syndrome |
| low birth-weight infant | premature labor |
| sore throat | skin problems |
| sleep disorders | stomach aches |

| stomach ailments | vaginal pain |
| ulcers | |

*Psychological Reactions*

| alcoholism | anorexia |
| anxiety attacks | bulimia |
| co-dependency | concentration difficulties |
| depression | drug abuse |
| flashbacks | lack of motivation |
| low self-esteem | memory loss |
| overeating | mistrust/dislike of |
| Post-Traumatic | opposite gender |
| Stress Disorder | relational problems |
| sexual disorders | gambling |

These effects are most severe for those abused by rankists. Yet, those who observe rankism are affected in much the same ways. The physical and psychological distress of witnessing a disturbing event is what Kaethe Weingarten called "common shock." All of her examples, with the exception of illness and death, are associated with rankism.[30]

Michael Marmot did a study of civil workers in Great Britain. His findings likely hold true for the United States. In his book, *The Status Syndrome*, Sir Marmot found that our health and longevity are due to more than genetics, diet, and technology. He found that the status we acquire with education, income, and titles does improve our lives, but that for a true sense of well being nothing can replace the control we feel over our lives or the participation we have in our social community.[31]

## Detail the Proposed Changes

No matter how effective our analysis of the situation and effects of rankism, if you do not propose specific alternatives, others may suggest you are a whiner.

As you propose what is to be changed, focus on behavior, and do not launch personal attacks, especially attacks against your perceived sense of someone's motivation. Moving individuals, groups, and organizations away from rankism toward right-rank can be difficult. If those involved feel personally attacked, they will dig in their heels and make the task even more arduous. True, you want to facilitate both outer and inner changes among the people involved, but begin by pointing to the need for changes "out there" and you will be more likely to find that the individuals will change themselves.

*Personal Behavior Changes.* A personal behavior change is one shift to propose. Do you want someone to stop shouting, to stop retreating into silence, to stop talking about you to others? Do you want the person to recognize you and call you by name, to be honest, rather than flatter you? By looking at the type of rankist you are dealing with, you can decide just what personal behavior is most rankist and how it needs to be changed.

*Structural Changes.* Structural changes are a second possible aim. Before you can suggest a change in the structure of an organization, you need to know how things work. That may mean looking at employee manuals, or the legal documents of your homeowners association, or the constitution of your service group. These can usually give insights as to why rankism is allowed to flourish.

Do you want your family to have weekly meetings? Do you want your partner or other family members to share household duties? Would you like to have required attendance at family evening meals? Do you want a board—rather than one Sovereign type—to oversee all workplace innovations? Do you want a by-laws change so that an increase in homeowner fees requires a 3/4-majority vote? Do you want a secure process for lodging complaints against rankists in your workplace? Do you want protection for whistleblowers?

*Attitude Changes.* Attitude changes among those in the rankist situation may be your goal. That means more than asking someone to be more positive. Attitudes are judgments we act on without thinking. If someone points out an attitude, we immediately recognize it as our own. Because humans once agreed, "The world is flat," they were careful to stay close to home, rather than risk falling over the edge.

As you detail proposed attitude changes, point to those that support rankism. Put each statement along an attitude scale that looks like this:

**Strongly Agree—Somewhat Agree—No Opinion— Somewhat Disagree—Strongly Disagree**

How do those involved judge these sorts of statements?
- Adults should tightly control children.
- Given the chance, all employees will steal.
- People are basically honest.
- Family problems are no one else's business.
- Keep workers on edge and they will produce more.
- Our worth depends on our income.
- Our worth depends on our education.
- Our worth depends on our political party.
- Good guys come in last.
- This service group exists for the board members.
- Only those who believe as we do deserve our help.
- The powerful obey laws differently than regular folk.
- The only reason for playing is to win.
- You are either with us OR against us.
- Good manners are old-fashioned.
- The haves and the have-nots; always had 'em always will.

You get the idea. Take a few steps away from the rankist situation, and come up with statements that support rankism that needs attitude changes.

Remember all the rankism in our society that was addressed only after attitudes had changed. No longer do most Americans agree with such statements as, "Negroes are inherently less intelligent," or "Women are too delicate to serve in the armed services," or "Father knows best."

## Decide on a Battle Plan

In his second book, *All Rise: Somebodies, Nobodies, and the Politics of Dignity*, Robert Fuller encourages us to make everyone accountable for the indignities they thrust on others.[32] Social pressure can be a powerful force for change. As you strive to stop rankism you can choose any of the following courses of action. Whether or not you have a specific rankist situation in mind, you can immediately begin the first action, "Take proactive steps." The way the next three actions are ordered, if one line of action works, your job is complete. If not, you can go on to the next. You can, of course, pursue any of these courses of action in any order you want. But it is nice to know that there are three other courses you can follow in the event that your first choice of action does not achieve the results you want.

Whatever direction you take, you need to temper your fear and be wary of your own and others' aggression to power. Mark Twain, the American philosopher, wrote, "Courage is resistance to fear, mastery of fear, not absence of fear." Yet, maybe we can reduce our trepidation of confronting a rankist. Tenzin Gyatso, the fourteenth Dalai Lama, has done some interesting work with American scientists. From his Buddist tradition, the Dalai Lama is convinced that meditation can alleviate fear and wanting. Scientists have recently shown that actions and contemplations, indeed, can physically change our brain.[33] That part of our brain called the amygdala, where we create our own fear, can be physically modified through mental training, so we decrease our fear.[34] Consider that treating a rankist with compassion can help you be less anxious. For each course of action proposed here you need to focus on your body, pay attention to your emotions, and tell yourself that you can handle this.

*Take Proactive Steps.* Following are four proactive steps you can take, beginning today, that comprise a course of action that will help stop rankism.

**Use rankism terms.** As you use these terms, realize some may be unfamiliar to others. You likely will need to explain terms and what rankism is all about. At the end of the book is a Glossary with rankism terms defined. By using such terms as "rankism" and "right-rank," you can increase the awareness of those involved in rankist situations. When I talked to people about this book, I found some immediately grasped these new ideas. Others needed more help becoming familiar with rankism.

**Recognize and credit examples of right-rank.** Not every Somebody is a rankist. Nor is everyone who challenges Somebodies a rankist. Descriptions of right-rank fill James Autry's book on caring leadership.[35] While you may not always have the authority to create an atmosphere of right-rank, you can recognize it when you observe it. When those closest to you or at work would rather partner with rather than control others, they are demonstrating right-rank.[36]

There are numerous examples of individuals who use their positions as parents, city mayors, or bosses to demonstrate their care and expertise. If you know of individuals who lead or follow or challenge while maintaining respect for all involved, give them credit. Why not offer "Right-Rank Awards" to those at your workplace who handled a particularly difficult situation with right-rank? Even if the concept of right-rank is not yet widely known, you can personally commend those who handle well their positions within a hierarchy.

*Support those who take assertive stands against rankism.* One of the reasons why rankists get away with their abuse is that no one challenges them. Where would the civil rights movement be today if the community had never acknowledged Rosa Parks for refusing to move to the back of the bus?

*Advance your own right-rank communication skills.* Often the reason rankism occurs is because those involved do not know of a better way to behave. Improved communication includes both knowledge and practice. We tend to use the same interpersonal practices as those around us. Sometimes, we mix with folks who are better communicators, and then our own repertoire of communication skills increases.[37] Find communication classes available through parks, libraries, community colleges, and other institutions. They are not only helpful, but also fun.

Interpersonal communication concentrates on interaction among persons with primary concern for each other's humanity. While we communicate, we move from being a speaker to a listener, from one who expresses to one who learns. Whether speaking or listening, we can use skills to improve the atmosphere of the interpersonal encounter by demonstrating our respect for the other person. Here are some pointers.

- Be positive and assume that things will turn out okay.
- Affirm others by recognizing them and showing your concern for their goals and interests.
- Reveal information they may not know.
- Own your own ideas and feelings.
- Attend to the conversational moment by putting everything else in the world aside for this important time you have together.

In the next section, you will find specific statements that can help you advance your communication skills as you work to stop rankism.

*Confer Directly with the Rankist.* It was a small cafe with four tables, and everyone was waiting for service. Just one woman was in charge, and she was taking orders, making the food, and delivering it to the tables. A tall man, accompanied by a short woman, stood at the counter and demanded immediate service. He wanted an ice cream cone for himself and a soft drink for her.

When the woman in charge explained to the customer that he would need to wait his turn, he began to berate her. What sort of place is this? Why open if you cannot take care of business? All I want is a cone and a drink! Surely, even you can manage that!

The woman in charge calmly explained there were others ahead of him and asked him to please wait for his turn.

Her response did not dissuade him. He became increasingly more abusive. The woman in charge never faltered, however, and she did eventually serve the tall man his cone and drink.

As they left, the short woman apologized to the woman in charge.

"He needs to learn respect," said the woman in charge.

Munching my lunch and watching this scenario, I wanted to stand and applaud the woman in charge. She was teaching us all how to tactfully confront a rankist.

Always begin—I am serious about this—always begin this course of action by conversing directly with the person who is misusing his or her rank. Too often we complain about rankism we endure to anyone who will listen—that is, to anyone except the abuser. Give that person a chance to recognize and change rankist behavior.

What if the person you plan to approach has an abrasive style and, predictably, will verbally attack you? Be ready! Decide how you will respond. It is possible to stand up to what Jay Carter called "nasty people" without mimicking their rancor or being drawn into their combative ways.[38] Remember, you have a right to express your discontent and you can do it in a direct and polite manner.

One reason why we avoid direct discussion with rankists is because we worry about how well we will handle the encounter. When emotionally distraught, we have all messed up. We may have said things we can never take back. We may have made a difficult situation worse. Harriet Lerner offered some suggestions about how to prepare ahead for such discussions. Most of her examples have to do with rankism.[39]

Marshall Rosenberg created a comprehensive approach to using thoughtful communication in stressful situations. He called it Nonviolent Communication because the strategies prevent participants from escalating discussions of serious differences into full-blown verbal and physical violence.[40]

*Approach Those Who Can Influence Change.* While it is our responsibility to challenge a rankist directly, we have no control over how that person will respond. Either way, it is right to first engage in face-to-face discussion with the rankist. If that does not work, and if rankism continues, going to someone who can affect a change may be your next, best course of action. If a clerk treats you badly, ask for the person's name and that of the supervisor.

Every instance of rankism occurs within a hierarchy. There is always someone who ranks higher than the rankist. In this country, no one has unrestricted power to abuse others. For example, even the President of the United States is accountable to someone and something greater than himself—the electorate and the checks and balances provided in the Constitution. Returning closer to home, go ahead and find out who your rankist answers to and what the superior's title is, then find out how you can contact him or her. Do not be discouraged if the supervisor is not readily available. Take the contact information and be persistent as you reach for right-rank.

When you know who to contact, gather your information and make an appointment, if appropriate. You will be less threatening if you meet at a time and place of their choosing. As you prepare for the meeting, take time to put together the parts of your presentation. Here is a proposed outline for your presentation to the person who can influence a change in a rankist situation.

1.   Mention a shared interest. The head honcho is committed to certain goals of which he or she is steward. Put yourself in that person's shoes. What does he or she want to accomplish, and how can you sympathize with those ambitions? Consider three settings—with a service club member, an airline employee, and a spouse in marriage counseling. These could be statements of shared interest.

   "We both want to see the Lion's Club build the new park."

   "We both depend on XXY Airlines to continue service here."

   "We both want this family to stay together."

2.   Do a situation audit. Begin by identifying some positive things to say about the situation, e.g., examples of right-rank. Then turn to the negative, instances of rankism. Remember: stick to descriptions of observed behavior. Some positive statements might be—

   "The purchasing committee has been working with a realtor."

   "Flights leave on time."

   "The younger kids are doing their household tasks."

Negative statements could be like these.

"The design committee has not met."

"Planes are only forty percent full."

"Donny, our oldest, is not doing his chores."

3. Propose a change. Rather than demand a change, put your proposal in the form of a request. Here are some examples.

"I want George, the chair, to include the rest of us in the design process."

"I wonder if we could put someone other than Meredith in charge of promotion and publicity?"

"I want Donny to be home on time and do his part."

Be prepared to describe the rankist behavior. You may not even have to get into the rankist behavior of the person; the rankist's superior may already know more than you can supplement. But if you are asked to specify the reasons, be ready. For example, you may be prepared with statements like these.

"George told me that he can do it better than a committee."

"Meredith says it isn't her problem."

"He's come home late a dozen times this month and leaves the garbage in the kitchen until it stinks."

4. Predict the results of the change. Since you know the circumstances and personal behavior so well by now, it is easy to show how a person or situation of right-rank will improve morale and participation among those involved. The more specific your predictions, the better. Without violating any confidence, quote those involved in the rankist situation or cite any of the reading sources listed in this chapter. Whatever the advantages you project, they should all lead the way for everyone involved to achieve their common goals. You could say something like these.

"The design will pass the full vote better if more
of us have input."
"Trish from St. Louis has turned around other
commuters."
"If Donny does his part, he'll be an example for
the other kids."

5.    Thank the person for any consideration they would offer
to improve the matter.

*Move to Activism.* In 2002, *Time* magazine named three
women as Persons of the Year. Cynthia Cooper informed the
board of WorldCom that massive fraud infested the company.
Colleen Rowley attempted to warn the head of the FBI about
Zacarias Moussaoui, who became a co-conspirator in the
September 11, 2001 bombings. Sherron Watkins sent a memo
to Kenneth Lay expressing her concerns about illegal accounting practices that were to become known as the Enron fraud.
Each tried to contact persons of influence and was basically
ignored. Sometimes, rankism is deeply entrenched and we
have no alternative other than to go public. Activism is the
final option.

Here are some who have gone public against rankism.
When Wynona Ward learned her brother had sexually abused
a girl, she decided, "It has to stop here. It can't keep going on."
This former woman truck driver, who was sexually abused by
her father, helped convict her brother. She finished her college
education while on the road, and in her mid-fifties, Wynona
went to law school. As a lawyer, she founded Have Justice
Will Travel to serve rural Vermont women too poor to come
to Ward's law office. So, she takes legal services to homes of
domestic violence. Wynona now employs two other attorneys
and a staff, all devoted to stomping out rankism.[41]

Kym Pasqualini, who survived an abduction, began an
organization that became the National Center for Missing
Adults. It is dedicated to the recovery of adults that law

enforcement consider to be endangered because of suspicious circumstances, physical or mental disabilities.

Perhaps, you will not need to start your own organization. Perhaps, a group that deals with the rankism that concerns you already exists. The general public was surprised when in spring of 2006, thousands of people, all over the country, marched against proposed Federal legislation that would criminalize undocumented immigrants and anyone who offered these people employment. Not everyone who marched agreed on the specifics of the proposed immigration law revisions. They did agree that their Senators and Representatives were crafting legislation that ignored the human dignity of a whole segment of people, regardless of how they came to the United States. The organizers of these marches worked quietly and effectively so that participants knew how to prepare, where to meet, and how to conduct themselves.

One way to start your search for an organization that supports your concerns about rankism is to contact Community Services in your town. Use the search engines available on the Internet to locate websites and "blogs," groups and organizations that share and/or act on your particular concerns. Ask anyone who might point you in the right direction.

Activism brings together constituencies who promote public awareness—usually with the help of media. It also engages the law against abusers who refuse to stop their rankism.

## Chapter Summary

As you create a plan for stopping rankism, take time to be well prepared. Look at the specific rankism situation that concerns you and identify the rankist behavior. Learn how to recognize and, if necessary, point out the effects of rankism. Determine exactly what changes you want to propose, and be prepared to provide the details. Then, choose your course of action.

If you are ready to begin, let us proceed. Do not worry if you are unable to change the world in a day. Everyone we touch who recognizes rankism in themselves and others, and who works to effect a change, makes an important difference. Together, we can make this a more decent world by reaching for right-rank.

### Reaching for Right-Rank: Your Plan for Stopping Rankism

To the strategy you created in Chapter Nine, add the information you devised from this chapter.

1. Identify the specific rankism situation.
2. Describe the rankist behavior.
3. Recognize the effects of rankism.
4. Detail the proposed change.
5. Decide on a course of action.
   a. Take proactive steps.
   b. Confer directly with the rankist.
   c. Approach those who can influence change.
   d. Move to activism.

# ACKNOWLEDGMENTS

Robert Fuller:        Writer and speaker, whose concept of rankism inspired this book and whose encouragement and specific comments on an early draft led to major changes—all for the better.

Rita van Alkemade:        Visual artist, whose grasp of my goal and whose illustrations surpassed my expectations.

Susannah Ortego:        Book editor, whose collegial manner brought us together as partners, and whose passion as both editor and potential reader smoothed my sometimes raggedy prose into a more readable book.

Bobbi Wambach:        Proofreader, who found two dozen more errors after several of us were done.

Lorraine Calbow:        Writer and storyteller, whose expertise and insights helped me refine the flow of *Battles*.

Bob and Sandy McCauley:        Friends, who opened their lives to include *Battles*.

| | |
|---|---|
| Michele DeFilippo and Ronda Rawlins: | 1106 Design, whose professional book design was executed with a sharp eye and graceful manner. |
| Middleton (WI) Senior Center: | Group of writers, who shared their own writing and generously offered suggestions for my publishing efforts. |
| Sun City Grand Book Club: | Readers, who presented both face-to-face feedback and margin notes in an early draft of *Battles*. |
| Noa Zanolli Davenport: | Co-author of *Mobbing: Emotional Abuse in the American Workplace*, whose generous advice both improved *Battles* and enlightened me on the promise and practicality of publishing and distributing my own manuscript. |
| David Altheide: | Scholar, whose perspectives on human interaction influenced me in *Battles* and in much of my other work. |
| Stephanie Heuer: | Author of *I Feel Like Nobody When… I Feel Like Somebody When…*, who consistently supported my work. |
| Bobby Walker: | Poet, who permitted me to include her poem "Power" in *Battles*. |

Finally, to all those who shared their battles with Somebodies and Nobodies, you have my deepest gratitude and respect, for without your openhearted accounts there would be no book.

# CHAPTER NOTES

## Preface

1. "Ethical Dilemma: What Would You Do?" ABC *Prime-Time Live*, Oct. 14, 2004.

2. Zogby International, September 2007. <www.zogby.com>

## Chapter 1

1. Lisabeth Mark, *Book of Hierarchies: A Compendium of Steps, Ranks, Orders, Links, Classes, Grades, Tiers, Arrays, Degrees, Lines, Divisions, Categories, Etc.* (New York: William Morrow & Co., 1984).

2. Lisa Guernsey, "Telling Tales Out of School," *New York Times*, May 8, 2003.

3. Stephanie Heuer, editor and narrator, Simon Goodway, illustrator, *I Feel Like Nobody When… I Feel Like Somebody When…* (Bloomingdale, Ind: AuthorHouse, 2005).

4. Joseph Epstein, *Snobbery: The American Version* (Boston: Houghton Mifflin, 2002), p. 18.

5. Alian DeButton, *Status Anxiety* (New York: Pantheon Books, 2004).

6. William A. Mason and Sally P. Mendoza (editors), *Primate Social Conflict* (Albany, NY: State University of New York Press, 1993).

7. Irving L. Janis, *Victims of Groupthink*, 2nd ed. (Boston: Houghton Mifflin, 1982).

8. Associated Press, "Documents Provide Details of Abuse Cases in Air Force Academy," *New York Times*, June 28, 2003.

9. Tonja R. Nansel, et al., "Cross-national Consistency in the Relationship Between Bully Behaviors and Psychosocial Adjustment," *Archives of Pediatrics & Adolescent Medicine*, Vol. 158, No. 8, August 2005.

10. American Association of University Women, "Drawing the Line: Sexual Harassment on the Campus." Graphic Communications, P.O. Box 7410, Gaithersburg, MD.

11. Robert W. Fuller, *Somebodies and Nobodies: Overcoming the Abuse of Rank* (Gabriola Island, BC, Canada: New Society Publishers, 2003), pp. 5–7.

12. Jim Sidanius and Felicia Piatto, *Social Dominance: An Intergroup Theory of Social Hierarchy and Oppression* (Cambridge, UK: Cambridge Press, 2001).

13. Joseph L. Graves, *The Emperor's New Clothes: Biological Theories of Race at the Millenium* (Piscataway, NJ: Rutgers University Press, 2003).

14. Robert H. Frank and Philip Cook, *The Winner-Take-All Society: Why a Few at The Top Get So Much More Than the Rest of Us* (New York: Free Press, 1995), pp. 15–16.

15. Rollo May, *Power and Innocence: A Search for the Sources of Violence* (New York: Norton, 1972), p. 21.

## Chapter 2

1. Robert M. Sapolsky and Lisa J. Share, "A Pacific Culture among Wild Baboons: Its Emergence and Transmission," *PLoS Biology*, Vol.2, No. 4 (April 2004). <plosbiology.org>.

2. Paul Avrich, *The Anarchists in the Russian Revolution* (Ithaca, NY: Cornell University Press, 1973).

3. Clifford Harper, *Anarchy, a Graphic Guide* (London, UK: Camden Press, 1987).

4. W. Edwards Deming, *Out of Crisis* (Cambridge, MA: MIT Press, 2000).

5. Bobby Walker, "Power," unpublished poem provided by the author.

6. Find information on the Dignitarian Foundation at <www.dignitarians.org>.

## Chapter 3

1. John Donne, "Meditation XVII."

2. Stories of over one hundred of the four hundred and fifty reported feral children can be found at <www.feralchildren.com>.

3. James Fennimore Cooper's "Autobiography of a Pocket Handkerchief" is out of print. The full text can be found at <cooper.thefreelibrary.com/Autobiography-of-a-Pocket-Handkerchief>.

4. Stuart Grassian, "Psychopathological Effects of Solitary Confinement," *American Journal of Psychiatry*, Vol. 140, November 1983, pp. 1450–1454.

5. Rene Gutel, "Biosphere 15 Years Later," KJZZ, National Public Radio, Feb. 14, 2006.

6. George Herbert Mead, *Mind, Self and Society* (Chicago: University of Chicago Press, 1934).

## Chapter 4

1. Robert H. Frank and Philip Cook, *The Winner-Take-All-Society: Why a Few at the Top Get So Much More Than the Rest of Us* (New York: Penguin, 1996).

2. Google Search.

3. Walter Kaufman (translator), Friedrich Wilhelm Nietzsche, *Beyond Good and Evil: Prelude to a Philosophy of the Future* (New York: Vintage Books, 1989), p. 259.

4. Douglas Smith (translator), Friedrich Wilhelm Nietzsche, *On the Genealogy of Morals: A Polemic: By Way of Clarification and Supplement to My Last Book Beyond Good and Evil* (Oxford, UK: Oxford University Press, 1999).

5. Walter Kaufman (translator), R. J. Hollingdale, Friedrich Wilhelm Nietzsche, *On the Genealogy of Morals/Ecce Homo* (New York: Vintage Books, 1989).

6. Alfred Adler, *The Individual Psychology of Alfred Adler: A Systematic Presentation in Selections From His Writing*. Edited and annotated by Heinz L. Ansbacher and Rowens R. Ansbacher (New York: Harper and Row, 1967), p. 103.

7. Adler, p. 115.

8. Adler, p. 103.

9. James Cross Giblin's *Life and Death of Adolf Hitler* (Boston: Clarion Books, 2002) is one of many fine books about Hitler.

10. "German Horror 'planned for a year,'" CNN, April 30, 2002, <cnn.com/WORLD/europe/04/30/erfurt.plan>.

11. Adler, p. 118.

12. Adler, p. 114.

13. Adler, p. 124.

14. Elizabeth Becker, "Pol Pot Remembered," *BBC News*, April 20, 1998.

15. Adler, p. 263.

16. Hannah Arendt, *Eichman in Jerusalem: A Report on the Banality of Evil* (New York: Penguin, 1994).

17. Primo Levi, *The Crowned and the Saved* (New York: Vintage, 1989).

## Chapter 5

1. Bonnie B. Strickland (editor), *Gale Encyclopedia of Psychology*, 2nd ed. (Farmington Hills, Mich.: Gale Group, 2001).

2. See Gavin DeBecker, *The Gift of Fear: Survival Signals That Protect Us from Violence* (New York: Little, Brown, 1997) for clues to using your intuition to save yourself.

3. Ronald M. Doctor and Ada P. Kahn, *The Encyclopedia of Phobias, Fears and Anxieties*, 2nd ed., (New York: Facts on File, Inc., 2000).

4. Eric Hoffer, *The Passionate Mind* New York: Harper & Row, 1968).

5. James T. Hamilton, *All the News That's Fit to Sell: How the Market Transforms Information into News* (Princeton, N.J.: Princeton University Press, 2003).

6. Bonnie Anderson, *News Flash: Journalism, Infotainment and the Business of Broadcast News* (San Francisco: Jossey-Bass, 2004).

7. David L. Altheide, *Creating Fear: News and the Construction of Crisis— Social Problems and Social Issues* (New York: Aldine de Gruyter, 2002).

8. Altheide, p. 3.

9. Altheide, pp. 26, 42.

10. "Trends in Violent Victimizations, 1973–2002," Bureau of Justice Statistics of the U. S. Department of Justice.

11. "Trends in Property Crime Victimizations, 1973–2002," Bureau of Justice Statistics of the U.S. Department of Justice.

12. "Uniform Crime Reports," Federal Bureau of Investigation Uniform Crime Reports, 2002.

13. Marshall McLuhan and Lewis H. Lapham, *Understanding Media: The Extensions of Man*, Reprint Edition (Cambridge, Mass.: MIT Press, 1994).

14. Anthony R. Pratkanis and Elliot Aronson, *Age of Propaganda: The Everyday Use and Abuse of Persuasion*, rev. ed. (New York: W. H. Freeman and Co., 2001).

15. Carl Jung, Gerhard Adler, and R.F.C. Hall, *Psychology and Alchemy* (Princeton, N.J.: Princton University Press, 1980).

16. Rollo May, *Power and Innocence: A Search for the Sources of Violence* (New York: Norton, 1972), p. 24.

## Chapter 6

1. Elizabeth Becker, "Pol Pot Remembered," *BBC News*, April 20, 1998.

2. Noa Zanolli Davenport, Ruth Distler Schwartz, and Gail Pursell Elliott, *Mobbing: Emotional Abuse in the American Workplace*, 3rd ed. (Collins, Iowa: Civil Society Publishing, 2005).

3. David Pelzer, *A Child Called"It": One Child's Courage to Survive* (Deerfield Beach, Fla.: Health Communications, 1995).

4. Edvard Radzinsky, *Stalin: The First In-Depth Biography Based on Explosive New Documents from Russia's Secret Archives* (Harpswell, Maine: Anchor, 1977), pp. 347–8.

5. Irving Janis, *Victims of Groupthink* (Boston: Houghton Mifflin, 1972) and Irving Janis, *Groupthink: Psychological Studies of Policy Decisions and Fiascos*, 2nd ed. (Houghton Mifflin, 1982).

6. Kevin McCoy, "Kozlowski borrowed $5M to buy ring," *USA Today*, Jan. 6, 2004.

7. Kevin McCoy, "Jury sees Kozlowski's Posh Digs via Video," *USA Today*, Nov. 25, 2003.

8. United States General Accounting Office, GOA/NSIAD-94-6, January 1994.

9. Jamie McIntyre, CNN, <www.cnn.com/2003/US/08/29/academy.assaults>.

10. "Japanese American Internment," <www.oz.net/~cyu/internment/timeline.html>.

11. Wen Ho Lee with Helen Zia, *My Country Versus Me: The First-Hand Account by the Los Alamos Scientist Who Was Falsely Accused of Being a Spy* (New York: Hyperion, 2001.) Dan Stober and Ian Hoffman, *A Convenient Spy: Wen Ho Lee and the Politics of Nuclear Espionage* (New York: Simon Schuster, 2001).

12. Associated Press, "U. S. Military to Expand Guantanamo Bay Camp," Aug. 26, 2003.

13. U.S. Department of Health and Human Services, Office of Research Integrity, National Institutes of Health, "Findings of Scientific Misconduct," June 19, 1999.

## Chapter 7

1. Rollo May, *Power and Innocence* (New York: Norton, 1972), p. 21.

2. Altina L. Waller, *Feud: Hatfields, McCoys, and Social Change in the Appalachia, 1860–1900* (Chapel Hill, N.C.: University of North Carolina, 1989).

3. John D. Aslant, Associated Press, "Nixon on Reagan: He 'just isn't pleasant to be around,'" *Salt Lake City Tribune*, Dec. 11, 2003.

4. Heinz Leymann's homepage <leymann.se/English/frame.html>. Also see Noa Zanolli Davenport, Ruth Distler Stewart, and Gail Pursell Elliott, *Mobbing: Emotional Abuse in the American Workplace*, 3rd ed. (Collins, Iowa: Civil Society Publishing, 2005).

5. For further information, see <madd.org/aboutus/o,1056,1686,00.html>.

6. "Suicide Mission," *Newsweek*, April 15, 2002.

7. Dennis Roddy, "Grant Street's Cybergossip," *Pittsburgh [PA] Post-Gazette*, Jan. 30, 1999, <post-gazette.com/columnists/19990130roddy5.asp>.

8. Lisa Guernsey, "Telling Tales Out of School," *New York Times*, May 8, 2003.

9. Robert K. Merton, "Social Structure and Anomie," *American Sociological Review*, Vol 3, (1938), pp. 672–682, 678.

## Part 4, Introduction

1. Karen Horney, *The Neurotic Personality of Our Times* (New York: Norton, 1937), p. 171.

## Chapter 9

1. Alfred Adler, *The Individual Psychology of Alfred Adler: A Systematic Presentation in Selections from His Writings*. Edited and annotated by Heinz L. Ansbacher and Rowens R. Ansbacher (New York: Harper & Row, 1967).

2. Karen Horney, *Our Inner Conflicts: A Constructive Theory of Neurosis* (New York: Norton, 1945).

3. Horney, pp. 49–62.

4. Horney, pp. 73–95

5. Horney, pp. 63–72.

6. Adler, pp. 126-171.

7. Alfred Adler, *Social Interest: Adler's Key to the Meaning of Life*, edited by Colin Brett, (Oxford, UK: Oneworld Publications, 1998), p. 207.

## Chapter 10

1. Elliott Aronson, *Nobody Left to Hate: Teaching Compassion after Columbine* (New York: Owl Books, 2001); Beverly B. Title, *Bully-Victim Conflict: An Overview for Educators* (Center City, Minn: Hazelden Foundation/Johnson Institute, 1995); Beverly Title and Lana S. Leonard, "Teaching Peace: The No-Bullying Program." Box 412, Hygiene, CA 85022. Internet: <info@teachingspace.org>.

2. Stephanie Heuer (ed. and narrator), Simon Goodway (illustrator), *I Feel Like Nobody When… I Feel Like Somebody When…* (Bloomingdale, Ind.: AuthorHouse, 2005).

3. Barbara Coloroso, *The Bully, the Bullied, and the Bystander: From Preschool to High School, How Parents and Teachers Can Help Break the Cycle of Violence* (New York: Harper Resource, 2003); Michael Thompson, Lawrence J. Cohen, and Catherine O'Neill Grace, *Mom, They're Teasing Me: Helping Your Child Solve Social Problems* (New York: Ballantine Books, 2002).

4. Ron Banks, "Bullying in Schools," ERIC Clearing House on Elementary and Early Childhood Education, No ED 407 154, Spring 2000.

5. Amy Harmon, "Internet Gives Teenage Bullies Weapons to Wound From Afar," *New York Times*, Aug. 26, 2004.

6. Rachel Simmons, *Odd Girl Out: The Hidden Culture of Aggression in Girls* (New York: Harvest Books, 2003).

7. Rosalind Wiseman, *Queen Bees and Wannabees: Helping Your Daughter Survive Cliques, Gossips, Boyfriends and Other Realities of Adolescence* (New York: Three Rivers Press, 2003).

8. Vern Seefeldt, "Understanding Sexual Harassment and the Abuse of Power in Athletic Settings," The Institute for the Study of Youth Sports, Michigan State University. Internet: <ed-web3.educ.msu.edu/ysi/spotlightfall98/understandsex.htm>.

9. Lila M. Cortina, et al., "Incivility in the Workplace: Incidence and Impact, *Journal of Occupational Health Psychology*, Vol. 6, No. 1, 2001, pp. 64–80.

10. Tim Field, *Bully in Sight: How to Predict, Resist, Challenge, and Combat Workplace Bullying* (Didcot, Oxfordshire, UK: Success Unlimited, 1996); Internet: <www.bullyonline.org>.

11. Chauncey Hare and Judith Wyatt, *Work Abuse: How to Recognize and Survive It* (Rochester, Vermont: Schenkman Books, 1997).

12. Richard V. Dennenberg and Mark Braverman, *The Violence-Prone Workplace: A New Approach to Dealing with Hostile, Threatening, and Uncivil Behavior* (Ithica, N.Y.: Cornell Univ. Press, 1999).

13. Noa Zanolli Davenport, Ruth Distler Schwartz, and Gail Pursell Elliott, *Mobbing: Emotional Abuse in the American Workplace*, 3rd ed. (Collins, Iowa: Civil Society Publishing, 2005).

14. Kathleen D. Ryan and Daniel K. Oestreich, *Driving Fear Out of the Workplace: Creating the High-Trust, High-Performance Organization*, 2nd ed. (San Francisco: Jossey-Bass, 1998).

15. Peter Block, *The Empowerment Manager: Positive Political Skills at Work* (San Francisco: Jossey-Bass, 1991).

16. Samuel Culbert and John B. Ullman, *Don't Kill the Boss! Escaping the Hierarchy Trap* (San Francisco: Berrett-Koehler, 2001).

17. Jim Collins, *Good to Great: Why Some Companies Make the Leap...and Others Don't* (New York: HarperCollins, 2001).

18. Ola W. Barnett, Cindy L. Miller-Perrin, and Robin D. Perrin, *Family Violence across the Lifespan: An Introduction* (Thousand Oaks, Calif.: Sage, 1996).

19. Alice Miller, Hunter Hannum, and Hildegarde Hannum, *For Your Own Good: Hidden Cruelty in Child-Rearing and the Roots of Violence*, 3rd ed. (New York: Farrar, Straus and Giroux, 1990).

20. Pamela J. Jenkins and Barbara Parmer Davidson, *Stopping Domestic Violence: How a Community Can Prevent Spousal Abuse* (New York: Kluwer Academic/Plenum Publishers, 2001).

21. Steven J. Wolin, *The Resilient Self: How Survivors of Troubled Families Rise Above Adversity* (New York: Villard, 1993).

22. Robert A. Becker, *Don't Talk, Don't Trust, Don't Feel: Overcoming the Power of Your Dysfunctional Family's Secrets* (Deerfield Beach, Fla: Health Communications, Inc, 1991).

23. Meg Kennery Dugan and Roger H. Hock, *It's My Life Now: Starting Over After an Abusive Relationship or Domestic Violence* (New York: Routledge, 2000).

24. Jan Yager, *When Friendship Hurts: How to Deal With Friends Who Betray, Abandon, or Wound You* (New York: Fireside, 2002).

25. Dawn Bradley Berry, *Domestic Violence Sourcebook*, 3rd ed. (Columbus, Ohio: McGraw-Hill, 2000).

26. Patricia Evans, *The Verbally Abusive Relationship: How to Recognize it and How to Respond*, 2nd ed. (Holbrook, Mass.: Bob Adams Inc., 1992).

27. Paul Hegstrom, *Angry Men and the Women Who Love Them: Breaking the Cycle of Physical and Emotional Abuse (Kansas City, Mo.*:Beacon Hill Press, 1999*);* Patricia Evans, *Controlling People: How to Recognize, Understand, and Deal with People Who Try to Control You Avon*, Mass.: (Adams Media Corporation, 2002); C. Terry Warner, *Bonds That Make Us Free: Healing Our Relationships, Coming to Ourselves* (Salt Lake City, Utah: Shadow Mountain, 2001); Beverly Engel, *The Emotionally Abused Woman: Overcoming Destructive Patterns and Reclaiming Yourself*, Reissued Edition, (New York: Ballantine, 1992).

28. Warren Farrell, "Spouse Abuse a Two-Way Street," *USA Today*, June 29, 1994; Armin A. Brott, "Special Supplement," *The Washington Post*, Dec. 28, 1993.

29. Though parts relate to only the United Kingdom, much of this book is applicable in the United States. Albert R. Roberts, *Handbook of Domestic Violence Intervention Strategies: Policies, Programs, and Legal* (Oxford, UK: Oxford University Press, 2002).

30. Kaethe Weingarten, *Common Shock* (New York: Dutton Books, 2003).

31. Michael Marmot, *The Status Syndrome: How Social Standing Affects Our Health and Longevity* (New York: Times Books, 2004).

32. Robert W. Fuller, *All Rise: Somebodies, Nobodies, and the Politics of Dignity* (San Francisco: Berrett-Koehler, 2006).

33. Samara Kalk, "Dalai Lama: Happiness Should Be Our Goal," *Capital Times* (Madison, WI) May 23, 2001.

34. Sharon Begley, *Train Your Mind, Change Your Brain* (New York: Ballantine Books, 2007), p. 233.

35. James A. Autry, *Love and Profit: The Art of Caring Leadership* (New York: Avon Trade Books, 1992).

36. Riane Eisler, *The Power of Partnership: The Seven Relationships That Will Change Your Life* (Novato, Calif.: New World Library, 2003.

37. Julie Ann Wambach, "Expressing and Learning: An Interpersonal Workshop."

38. Jay Carter, *Nasty People: How to Stop Being Hurt by Them Without Becoming One of Them* (Columbus, Ohio: Barnes and Noble Books, 2002).

39. Harriet Lerner, *The Dance of Connection: How to Talk to Someone When You're Mad, Hurt, Scared, Frustrated, Insulted, Betrayed, or Desperate* (New York: HarperCollins, 2001).

40. Marshall B. Rosenberg, *Nonviolent Communication: A Language of Life*, 2nd ed. (Encinitas, CA: PuddleDancer Press, 2003).

41. "Have Justice Will Travel," PBS *Now*, Mar. 14, 2008.

# GLOSSARY

Abuse:
To promote oneself or one's interest while bringing harm to another person or community.

Activist:
Overt Nobody type of right-rank who uses social organization to attack rankism.

Adler, Alfred:
An early twentieth-century psychologist who was interested in how humans seek power, and how they use that power either to help society or as rankists to help only themselves.

Aggressive posture:
A conflict posture where we move against those who threaten us.

Alpha:
The first letter of the Greek alphabet, used in this context to denote a dominant member of a group.

Anarchist:
Type of overt Somebody Rankist who seeks to overthrow governments in the hope that everyone will then live in equal harmony, but with no plan to reorganize society. Historically this has always led to violent disorder and mayhem.

| | |
|---|---|
| Anxiety: | Generalized fear that can paralyze a person who is facing no real threat. |
| Avenger: | Type of covert Nobody Rankist who strikes at a Somebody Rankist in such a way that the Avenger will not be recognized. |
| Bully: | Takes advantage of the weaker by treating them in a variety of rankist ways so the recipient feels threatened and humiliated. See Tim Fields online at *www.bullyingonline.org*. |
| Common shock: | Term coined by Kaethe Weingarten that describes the effect on those who observe rank abuse of others. |
| Communication: | Used here to describe the process by which we interact with others to make sense of our physical and social world, as well as of our Self. |
| Compliant posture: | Conflict posture where we move toward those who threaten us. |
| Conflict postures: | Ways in which we orient ourselves against those who may attack us. |
| Covert: | Behavior that is less public or more subtle or hidden, less easily observed. |
| Detached posture: | Conflict posture where we move away from those who threaten us. |
| Dignitarian Foundation: | Inspired by Robert Fuller, a foundation associated with the Dignity Movement, which promotes respectful treatment of all persons—regardless of their economic, educational, or social rank. See website *www.dignitarians.org*. |
| Dog-Kicker: | Type of overt Nobody Rankist who strikes back at abuse from a superior by attacking someone who is weaker. |

| | |
|---|---|
| Degree of activity: | Alfred Adler's suggestion that the amount of activity each rankist and right-rank type directs toward others in a hierarchy helps us understand the person's social concern. |
| Emotional abuse: | One of the results of rankism is emotional damage to the participants. |
| Empathy: | Process of understanding others by putting ourselves in their bodies and minds so we can learn what it means to be human. |
| Extortionist: | Type of overt Somebody Rankist who takes advantage of those under the Extortionist's tutelage by making demands that are unreasonable and demeaning. |
| Fabricator: | Type of covert Somebody Rankist who pretends to create and distribute items or services, but who actually distributes falsehoods or the credible work of others as the Fabricator's own. |
| Feral children: | Youngsters who have lived in solitude, away from human contact and are later unable to become social beings. |
| Flatterer: | Type of overt Nobody Rankist who insincerely compliments the rank abuser in hopes of being spared from the rankist's abuse. |
| Fuller, Robert: | An academic and author who coined the word "rankism" in his book *Somebodies and Nobodies: Overcoming the Abuse of Rank*. |
| Gangster: | Type of overt Somebody Rankist who encourages others to gang up on one Nobody and drive that person out. |

Gatekeeper:

Type of covert Somebody Rankist who permits or denies access to people, information or opportunities in order to control individuals and the system.

Gossip:

Type of covert Nobody Rankist who undermines others by spreading uncomplimentary stories that may or may not be true.

Grandee:

Type of overt Somebody Rankist who misuses people and systems because Grandees treat everything as though it belongs to them and the rules do not apply to them.

Hierarchy:

Any network of humans where some rank higher and others rank lower.

Horney, Karen:

Twentieth-century psychologist who was interested in how some humans desire unreasonable control over others. According to Horney, when dealing with power, individuals move toward, away or against others.

Integrative posture:

Conflict posture where we move among conflict participants.

Maslow, Abraham H.:

Psychologist who proposed a hierarchy of needs in which our physical needs must be met before we can grow into love, esteem, and self-actualization.

Mead, George Herbert:

Proposed that our self-identity is created through our interaction with others, and that together we create who each of us is.

Mobbing:

Heinz Leymann's term for the way superiors, coworkers, or even subordinates gang-up on someone to

| | |
|---|---|
| | drive them out. The Gangster-type Somebody Rankists acts in much the same fashion. |
| Nietzsche, Friedrich W.: | Eighteenth-century German philosopher who believed that the "will to power" was instinctive and that morality was different for upper and lower classes. |
| Noble Sufferer: | Type of covert Nobody Rankist who projects self as a martyr, rather than trying to fight the rankism. |
| Nobody givers: | Nobodies with high social concern and high activity who give to society, rather than take from it. |
| Nobody Rankist: | Retaliates against mistreatments of the powerful with rebellion and sometimes with violence. |
| Nobody receivers: | Nobodies with low activity and either high or low social concern, who would rather receive than give or take. |
| Nobody takers: | Nobodies with high activity and low social concern who take from society, rather than give. |
| Omega: | The last letter of the Greek alphabet, used in this context to refer to those within a hierarchy without power. |
| Onlooker: | Type of covert Nobody Rankist who stops participating, but does not walk away from or try to change the rankism. |
| Ordination: | Horney's classification of one's movement related to another—toward, away, against; plus Wambach's ordination of integrative. |

| | |
|---|---|
| Overt: | Behavior that is public, blatant, obvious. |
| Persuader: | Overt Nobody type of right-rank who appeals to rankists and others in the conflict situation to stop abuse. |
| Phobia: | A fear of something specific in the absence of any present threat, a condition that can incapacitate a person. |
| Placater: | Type of covert Nobody Rankist who is willing to be conciliatory because of a desire for peace at any cost. |
| Rankism: | The abuse of position within a hierarchy from both up and down the lines of power. |
| Rankist: | One who misuses a position within a hierarchy to abuse others. |
| Rank: | One's level above or below others because of title, occupation, or social position. |
| Rank Conflict Inventory: | A self-inventory that helps identify individual patterns of possible rankism. |
| Retaliator: | Type of overt Nobody Rankist who strikes back in kind. |
| Right-rank: | Use of one's position to better individuals and society by showing respect for the human dignity of everyone. |
| Scapegoater: | Type of covert Somebody Rankist who transfers personal blame to weaker persons or groups. |
| Seething Giant: | Type of overt Somebody Rankist who controls others with intense physical and verbal outbursts that cannot be predicted. |

| | |
|---|---|
| Self: | A process whereby, according to George Herbert Mead, we realize that others treat us as objects and that together, we and they define one another. |
| Snobs: | Those who use objects to increase their own social importance at the expense of others. |
| Snubber: | Type of covert Somebody Rankist who treats those of lower rank with indifference, as though they do not exist. |
| Social conflict: | Conflict within social groups that can be productive and move members toward improvements, or conflict that can be detrimental and hurt individuals and group goals. Rankism leads to negative and disruptive conflicts. |
| Social hierarchy: | Necessary arrangement of all human gatherings, so we can work together and live peaceably. |
| Social concern: | Motivation for behavior intended to better individuals' lives and society as a whole. |
| Somebody Rankist: | One who protects a superior position by obstructing anyone of lesser power. |
| Somebody receivers: | Somebodies with low activity and low social concern who receive, rather than give or take. |
| Somebody takers: | Somebodies with low social concern and high activity who take from the world, rather than give to it. |
| Sovereign: | Type of overt Somebody Rankist who maintains control by rewarding only those who are unquestioningly loyal. |

| | |
|---|---|
| Status: | The importance others attribute to a person regardless, and sometimes in spite of, the person's rank. |
| Tenzin Gyatso: | Fourteenth Dalai Lama. |
| Tyrant: | Type of overt Somebody Rankist who intimidates others with a steely, unemotional presence followed by harsh discipline. |
| Verbal abuse: | Attacks of emotion-laden words that can be as damaging as physical blows. |

# ABOUT THE AUTHOR

Dr. Julie Ann Wambach mediates disputes for a variety of nonprofit and governmental entities. She has long been interested in the dynamics of power in every human interaction. When Julie read Robert Fuller's *Somebodies and Nobodies*, she knew immediately that rankism is a communication problem. She determined to write a book that offered communication alternatives to rank abuse.

After receiving a B.S. degree from the University of Wisconsin-Madison, Julie taught high school speech communication and English for 5 years. She later completed her M.A. in Speech Communication and Ph.D. in Adult Development and Aging at Arizona State University. As Professor of Human Communication at Scottsdale [Arizona] Community College, she published two textbooks and numerous articles appearing in juried academic journals and professional magazines.

She has spoken to and led workshops at professional conferences and before college, community, government, political, and religious groups. She has counseled individuals and married couples, and has been a speechwriter, coach, and editor for business leaders and elected officials. She has worked as a community activist for the environment, the elderly, and political candidates. You can reach Julie at *right-rank.com*.

# INDEX

193